Common CORE Comprehension

Practice at 3 Levels ●●●

Table of Contents

Using This Book 2

Overview I • Introduction to Narrative Texts 6

Unit 1: Memoirs Mini-Lesson 8
   Memoirs I 10
   Memoirs II 14
Unit 2: Historical Fiction Mini-Lesson 18
   Historical Fiction I 20
   Historical Fiction II. 24
Unit 3: Myths/Legends Mini-Lesson 28
   Myths. 30
   Legends. 34
Unit 4: Science Fiction Mini-Lesson 38
   Science Fiction I 40
   Science Fiction II. 44

Overview II • Introduction to Informational Texts 48

Unit 5: Informational Texts: Social Studies Mini-Lesson 50
   Ancient Civilizations 52
   Geography 56
   Economics 60
   Government and Citizenship 64
Unit 6: Informational Texts: Science Mini-Lesson 68
   Life Science: Ecology 70
   Environmental Science 74
   Physical Science: Forces and Motion 78
   Earth Science: Energy 82

Overview III • Introduction to Opinions/Arguments 86

Unit 7: Persuasive Essays Mini-Lesson. 88
   Persuasive Essays I. 90
   Persuasive Essays II 94
Unit 8: Book and Film Reviews Mini-Lesson 98
   Book Reviews 100
   Film Reviews 104
Unit 9: Advertisements Mini-Lesson 108
   Advertisements I 110
   Advertisements II 114
Unit 10: Speeches Mini-Lesson 118
   Speeches I 120
   Speeches II 124

Answer Key 128

Using This Book

What Is the Common Core?

The Common Core State Standards are an initiative by states to set shared, consistent, and clear expectations of what students are expected to learn. This helps teachers and parents know what they need to do to help students. The standards are designed to be rigorous and pertinent to the real world. They reflect the knowledge and skills that our young people need for success in college and careers.

What Are the Intended Outcomes of Common Core?

The goal of the Common Core Standards is to facilitate the following competencies. Students will:

- demonstrate independence;
- build strong content knowledge;
- respond to the varying demands of audience, task, purpose, and discipline;
- comprehend as well as critique;
- value evidence;
- use technology and digital media strategically and capably;
- come to understand other perspectives and cultures.

What Does This Mean for You?

If your state has joined the Common Core State Standards Initiative, then as a teacher you are required to incorporate these standards into your lesson plans. Your students may need targeted practice in order to meet grade-level standards and expectations, and thereby be promoted to the next grade. This book is appropriate for on-grade-level students as well as intervention, ELs, struggling readers, and special needs students. To see if your state has joined the initiative, visit http://www.corestandards.org/in-the-states.

What Does the Common Core Say Specifically About Reading?

For reading, the Common Core sets the following key expectations.

- Students must read a "staircase" of increasingly complex texts in order to be ready for the demands of college or career-level reading.
- Students must read a diverse array of classic and contemporary literature from around the world, as well as challenging informational texts in a range of subjects.
- Students must show a "steadily growing ability" to comprehend, analyze, and respond critically to three main text types: Opinion/Argument, Informational, and Narrative.

Common Core Comprehension Grade 6 • ©2012 Newmark Learning, LLC

How Does This Book Help My Students?

Common Core Comprehension offers:

- **Three leveled, reproducible versions of each passage** are provided so that below-grade-level students start their comprehension practice at their reading level. Repeated readings and teacher support scaffold students up to the on-grade-level passage. Struggling students do not miss out on essential comprehension practice because the comprehension questions can be answered no matter which passage is read. The Common Core Standards require students to progress to grade-level competency. Therefore, it is recommended that once students build background on the topic, they staircase up to the on-grade-level passage, which includes richer vocabulary and language structures.

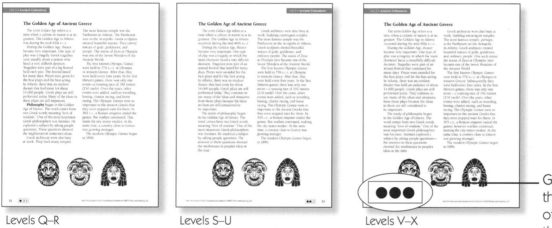

Levels Q–R   Levels S–U   Levels V–X

Gives the teacher the reading level of each of the three passages. See the chart on page 5.

- **An Overview page** introduces each of the three sections and provides background on the text type and genres in that section. A graphic organizer is provided to help you introduce the text type.

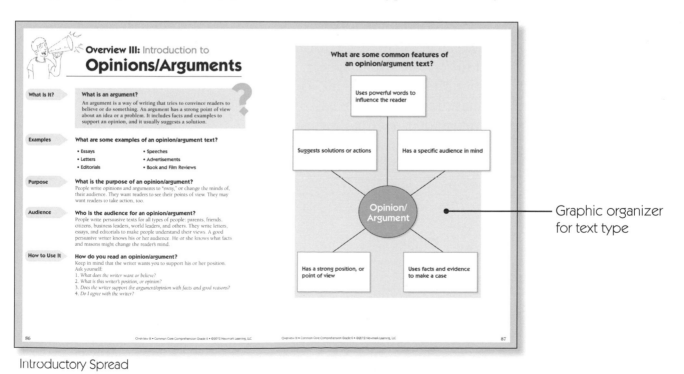

Graphic organizer for text type

Introductory Spread

- **Each set of passages in a genre begins with a mini-lesson** that consistently frames the specific details of the genre students are about to read. A reproducible graphic organizer is provided for you to share as is, or you can cover the answers and complete together or individually as a response to your mini-lesson.

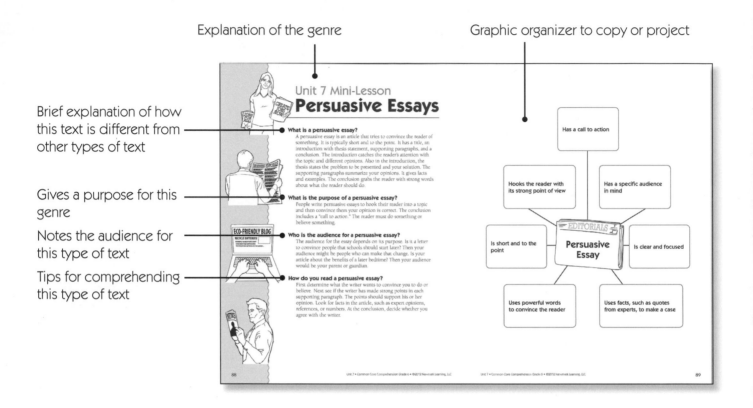

Explanation of the genre

Graphic organizer to copy or project

Brief explanation of how this text is different from other types of text

Gives a purpose for this genre

Notes the audience for this type of text

Tips for comprehending this type of text

- **Text-dependent and critical-thinking questions** appear after each set of passages. The questions are research based and support the Common Core reading standards at grade level.

- **Students get rich text type and genre practice** using an array of narrative texts, content-area informational texts in social studies and science, and opinion/argument texts, as per the Common Core Standards.

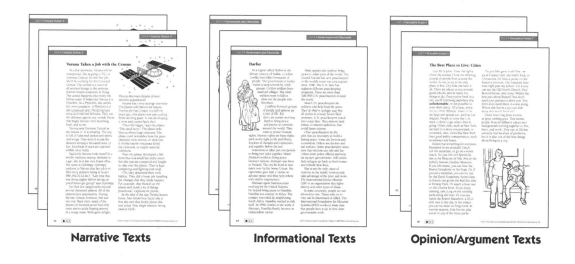

Narrative Texts   **Informational Texts**   **Opinion/Argument Texts**

- **Vocabulary is studied in context,** as per the Common Core Standards.

place to live. City kids can have it all. There are places to run around, good schools, and so many fun things to do. Once you've lived in a city, you'll find living anywhere else **unfathomable**, or not possible to even think about. Of course, every city is a little different. Some cities are large and spread out, such as Los An...

runs right past my school. On it you can see the Old North Church, Paul Revere's house, and more. What's the best part about Boston? You don't need your parents to drive you. You don't even need them to come along. Where else but in a city can kids enjoy this much freedom?

Cities have long been known ... melting ...

How Are the Passages Leveled?

The first passage is two grades below level, the second passage is one grade below level, and the third passage is on grade level. Please refer to the chart below to see a correlation to letter levels and number levels.

Common Core Practice Reading Levels

Level Icon	Grade 1		Grade 2		Grade 3		Grade 4		Grade 5		Grade 6	
●○○	A–C	1–4	D–E	5–8	F–I	9–16	L–M	24–28	N–P	30–38	Q–R	40
●●○	D–E	5–8	F–I	9–16	J–M	18–28	N–P	30–38	Q–R	40	S–U	44–50
●●●	F–I	9–16	J–M	18–28	N–P	30–38	Q–R	40	S–U	44–50	V–X	60

Overview I: Introduction to Narrative Texts

What Is It?

What is a narrative text?

A narrative text is a real or fiction story that follows a story structure. That structure leads with capturing the reader's attention. The story then gives details about the characters, setting, and the plot. Usually a problem will arise and actions will be taken that lead to a solution of the problem. This gives rise to the conclusion, which should satisfy the reader's interest and answer the reader's questions as much as possible.

Examples

What are some examples of a narrative text?

- Narrative Fiction
- Realistic Fiction
- Fairy Tales
- Fables
- Myths and Legends
- Science Fiction
- Fantasy
- Historical Fiction
- Narrative Nonfiction
- Biographies
- Memoirs
- Journals and Diaries

Purpose

What is the purpose of a narrative text?

Basically, the purpose is to tell a story. Different types of narratives will have different purposes. For example, the purpose of a fable is to teach people lessons or explain mysteries of Earth.

Audience

Who is the audience for a narrative text?

The audience is any reader of that text. Though many people prefer certain types of narrative text more than others, the stories are meant to interest anyone. Sometimes you will enjoy a book because you relate to a character, a setting, or a problem in the book. Other times you will enjoy a story that is told really well, even though the story line is not your favorite.

How to Use It

How do you read a narrative text?

Since narrative texts follow a sequence, they should be read from beginning to end. Use a graphic organizer or highlighter to keep the characters straight in the beginning. Do research on real-life settings, if they are unfamiliar. For example, if the characters are on an African safari, perhaps look at some books or websites on safaris and Africa. Understanding the world of the characters makes it easier to immerse yourself in the story.

What are some common features of a narrative text?

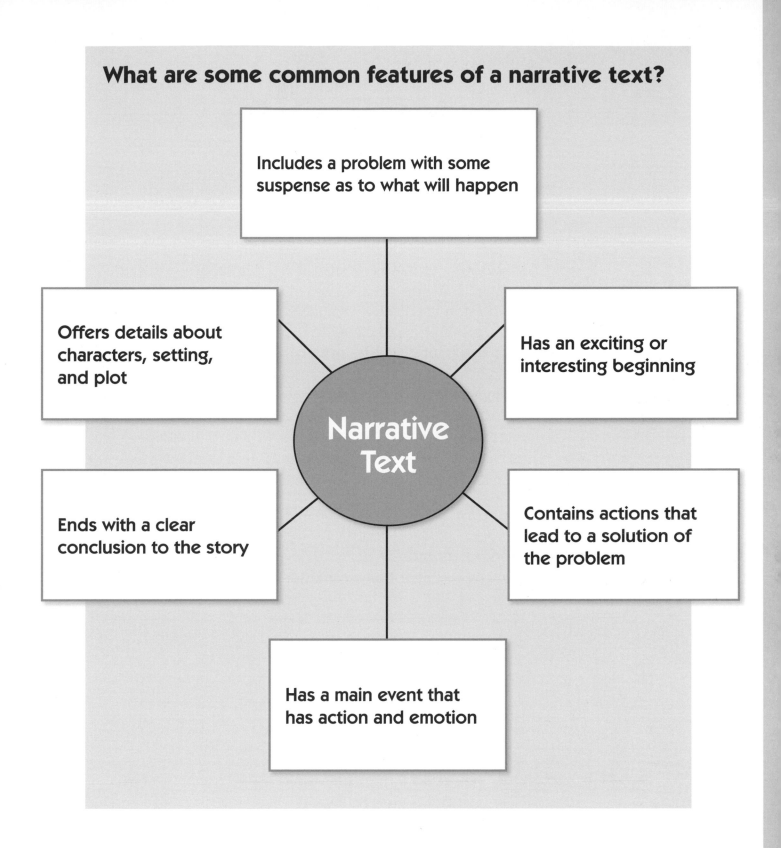

Includes a problem with some suspense as to what will happen

Offers details about characters, setting, and plot

Has an exciting or interesting beginning

Narrative Text

Ends with a clear conclusion to the story

Contains actions that lead to a solution of the problem

Has a main event that has action and emotion

Memoirs

What is a memoir?

A memoir is writing that covers a short period of time in the life of the person writing it. Memoirs focus on the events, thoughts, and feelings of that person. They are often about a specific time or place or a moment in history that is important to the writer. Memoirs communicate the conflict and drama of events with a strong, personal point of view.

What is the purpose of a memoir?

The purpose of a memoir is to describe events as the writer remembers them. These writers want to share their experiences with the rest of the world. Some writers may have lived through important times or contributed to world-changing events. They want readers to know what they did and to share what they felt. Writers may also use the memoir as a journey of self-discovery. Writing about the past can help people better understand themselves and how they came to be who they are.

Who writes memoirs?

In the past, people who took part in world-changing events, like explorations or scientific discoveries, wrote memoirs. The writers wanted to give an eyewitness account of the event. But memoirs are not always about major or public events. You don't have to be famous to write a memoir! People today often write memoirs because a period of time in their lives was important to them. Memoirs can be about everyday events. They are interesting to readers because of the way the writer remembers and explains the events.

How do you read a memoir?

When you read a memoir, you are reading a first person narrative: one person's memory of an event or time. Enter into the moment with the writer. Try to picture yourself there. Think about what is important and why the writer chose to write about the event. Look for insight into why it was important to the writer. The writer remembered the moment in great detail.

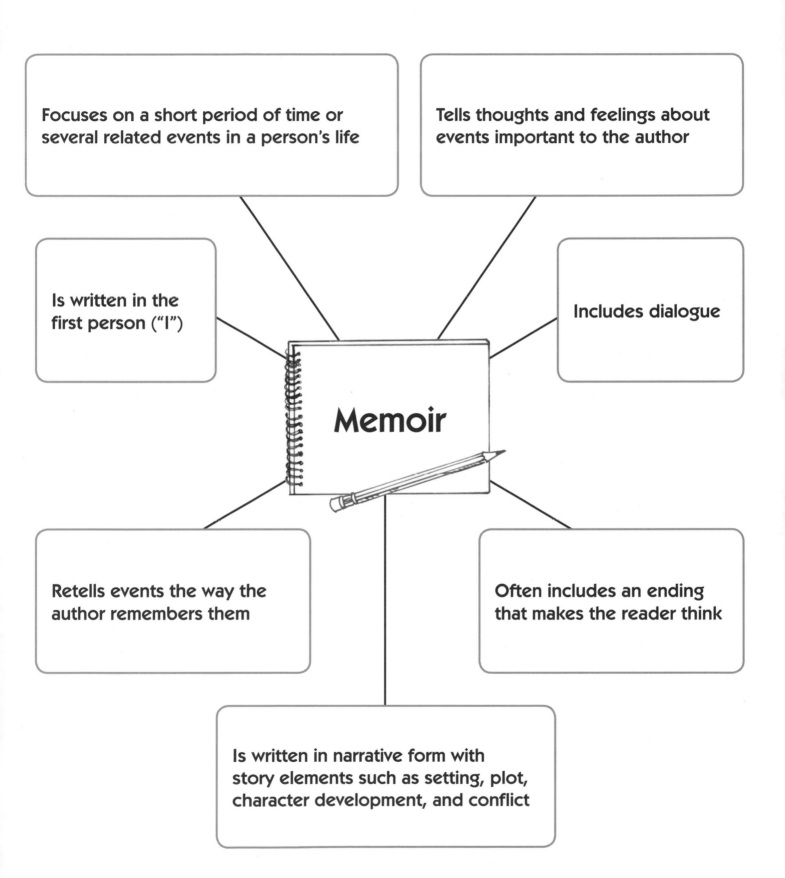

Focuses on a short period of time or several related events in a person's life

Tells thoughts and feelings about events important to the author

Is written in the first person ("I")

Includes dialogue

Memoir

Retells events the way the author remembers them

Often includes an ending that makes the reader think

Is written in narrative form with story elements such as setting, plot, character development, and conflict

"We Shall Not Be Moved"

I am who I am because of my grandfather. It is because of Grandpa David that I marched for civil rights. He taught me that discrimination is wrong. Because of him, I do not judge people by how they look. He is also why I have friends from different cultures.

I was born in 1944. At that time, Grandpa David Greenspan lived with my parents. We lived on Bolton Street in the Bronx. The Bronx is a part of New York City. Grandpa David was born in Poland. He left Poland in 1910 because he did not want to fight in the army. Grandpa believed in peace.

Grandpa was an open-minded person. He did not judge people. He once brought a homeless man home to our little apartment. From then on, this man would come over every Tuesday night for dinner. I learned a lot from Grandpa's actions. His kindness to others taught me the right way to treat people.

Stokely Carmichael was one of my best friends in school. Stokely later became an activist. We were in high school in the late 1950s. At that time, in America, the civil rights movement was on everyone's mind. A few years earlier, the Supreme Court said it was against the law to separate people by **race** or color of their skin. But **segregation**, or separating people based on race, was still happening in many places. Stokely began participating in demonstrations around New York

City. A demonstration is when you get people to support a cause. He joined the Freedom Riders. I joined the National Conference of Christians and Jews. It's an organization focused on peace and tolerance.

Many businesses were discriminating against people. They would not give jobs to people of other races. Early one Saturday morning when I was thirteen, I went to protest at the department store Macy's. The store wouldn't hire African Americans. A crowd of people from different backgrounds carried signs that said "Jobs Now!" and "Full Employment!"

We marched and sang protest songs like "We Shall Not Be Moved."

Music was a big part of the civil rights movement. Singer-songwriters such as Pete Seeger, Joan Baez, and Bob Dylan used traditional folk music to create popular protest songs. In 1964, President Lyndon Johnson passed the Civil Rights Act. This was an order making it illegal to discriminate against anyone on the basis of race, color, religion, sex, or national origin.

The sum of a person is more than her parts. If I were an equation, it might look like this: Grandpa David + Civil Rights + Music = Me.

We Shall Not Be Moved

My Grandpa David is my role model. He is the reason I marched for civil rights. He is why I think discrimination and prejudice are wrong. He is why I've made friends from different cultures.

When I was born in 1944, Grandpa David Greenspan was living with my mother and father in the Bronx. The Bronx is a part of New York City. He had left his Polish homeland as a young man in 1910 because he did not want to fight in the army. Grandpa believed in peace, not war.

Grandpa was a very accepting and open-minded person. Once he came home to our little apartment on Bolton Street with a homeless man. From then on, this man would come over every Tuesday night for dinner. It was through my Grandpa's actions, his kindness to others, and uncompromising humanity that I learned the right way to treat people.

One of my closest friends in high school was Stokely Carmichael. Stokely later became a leader of an activist organization. It was the late 1950s. At that time, the civil rights movement was sweeping across America. A few years earlier, the Supreme Court had declared that separating people on the basis of race was illegal. But segregation and inequality still existed in many places. Stokely began taking part in demonstrations around New York City. A demonstration is when you get people to support a cause. He joined the Freedom Riders. I joined the National Conference of Christians and Jews. That is an organization that promotes peace and tolerance in a world of diversity.

Despite what the law said, many businesses still discriminated. They would not offer jobs to people of other races. Early one Saturday morning when I was thirteen, I went to picket, or protest, at Macy's. They wouldn't hire African Americans. A crowd of people from different backgrounds carried picket signs that said "Jobs Now!" and "Full Employment!" We marched and sang protest songs like "We Shall Not Be Moved."

Music was an important part of the civil rights movement. Singer-songwriters such as Pete Seeger, Joan Baez, and Bob Dylan drew heavily from traditional folk music and popularized protest songs. In 1964, President Lyndon Johnson passed an executive order called the Civil Rights Act. The order made it illegal to discriminate against anyone on the basis of race, color, religion, sex, or national origin.

The sum of a person is more than her parts. But if I were an equation, it might look like this: Grandpa David + Civil Rights + Music = Me.

We Shall Not Be Moved

My Grandpa David is my role model. He is the reason I marched for civil rights, why I think discrimination and prejudice are wrong, and why I've made friends from different cultures.

When I was born in 1944, Grandpa David Greenspan was living with my mother and father in the Bronx. The Bronx is a part of New York City. He had left his Polish homeland as a young man in 1910 because he did not want to fight in the army. Grandpa believed in peace, not war.

Grandpa was a very accepting and open-minded person. Once he came home to our little apartment on Bolton Street in the Pelham Parkway section with a homeless man. From then on, this man would come over every Tuesday night for dinner. It was through my Grandpa's actions, his kindness to others, and uncompromising humanity that I learned the right way to treat people.

One of my closest friends in school was Stokely Carmichael, a future leader of an activist organization. We were in high school in the late 1950s. At that time, the civil rights movement was sweeping across America. A few years earlier, the Supreme Court had declared that separating people on the basis of race was illegal. But segregation and inequality still existed in many places. Stokely began participating in demonstrations around New York City. A demonstration is when you get people to support a cause. He joined the Freedom Riders. I joined

the National Conference of Christians and Jews. That is an organization dedicated to promoting peace and tolerance in a world of diversity.

Despite what the law said, many businesses still discriminated. They would not offer jobs to people of other races. Early one Saturday morning when I was thirteen, I went to picket, or protest, at Macy's because they wouldn't hire African Americans. A crowd of people from different backgrounds carried picket signs that said "Jobs Now!" and "Full Employment!" We marched and sang protest songs like "We Shall Not Be Moved."

Music was an important part of the civil rights movement. Singer-songwriters such as Pete Seeger, Joan Baez, and Bob Dylan drew heavily from traditional folk music and popularized protest songs. In 1964, President Lyndon Johnson passed the Civil Rights Act. This was an executive order making it illegal to discriminate against anyone on the basis of race, color, religion, sex, or national origin.

The sum of a person is more than her parts. But if I were an equation, it might look like this: Grandpa David + Civil Rights + Music = Me.

Name _____ Date _____

Use what you read in the passage to answer the questions.

1. What does the word **segregation** mean?

_____

_____

2. What year was the writer born?

_____

_____

3. What clue in the passage helps you infer that Grandpa David did not believe in fighting?

_____

_____

4. What kind of person was Grandpa David? Use clues in the text to support your answer.

_____

_____

5. Who is Stokely Carmichael and why does the writer mention him?

_____

_____

6. Show your understanding of the word **race** by naming a race?

_____

_____

7. How was Macy's breaking the law?

_____

_____

8. The writer is a person who takes action. What clues help you draw this conclusion?

_____

_____

A New Beginning

In the years before I started high school, I wasn't very good at . . . well, anything. For instance, I wasn't any good at playing baseball. When my friends chose up sides for a ball game, I was always the last one to get picked.

I wasn't any good at hide-and-go-seek. When I closed my eyes to count to one hundred, I think my friends just went home.

Playing tag wasn't any better for me. When I was tagged and was *it*, I stayed *it*. As far as I know, I'm still *it*.

And when I got a little older and it came to girls, forget about it. I figured I was as interesting to girls as a fire hydrant. Across the hall from our apartment lived Mary. Mary was the prettiest girl in the world. The problem was that Mary dated older boys who slicked their hair back and wore black leather jackets.

The only thing I was any good at was reading. I liked to read books, such as Ian Fleming's James Bond novels, techno thrillers, science fiction, the Hardy Boys books, and Sherlock Holmes detective stories.

In September 1963, everything changed for me. I started high school. I wanted to go to the nearby high school with the neighborhood kids. But my English teacher, Sister Elizabeth, had other ideas. She wanted me to attend Cardinal Spellman High School, a **scholarship** high school only kids with good grades could attend.

"At Spellman you'll get a better education," Sister Elizabeth said, "and you'll be better prepared for college." My future was cast!

When I started going to classes at Spellman, I met lots of kids like me— boys and girls who were smart and good at reading. Nobody cared that I stank at baseball, hide-and-go-seek, and tag.

I joined the Spellman marching band and learned to play the clarinet. Every day after school we had band practice. And at practice, I couldn't keep my eyes off a pretty blond freshman named Cathy who sat nearby playing the saxophone. When I looked at her, she smiled at me.

One afternoon after practice, Cathy and I walked out of the band room at the same time.

"The school dance is this Friday night," she said to me. "Wanna go to the dance with me?" Cathy asked.

"Okay." That was all I could say. I was astonished. Cathy wrote her address on a slip of paper and gave it to me. I looked at the address and noticed her street wasn't far from school.

"Can I walk you home?" I asked with my heart pounding.

"Sure."

Cathy and I happily chatted all the way to her house. And later that week, we went to the school dance!

A New Beginning

In the years before I started high school, I wasn't very good at . . . well, anything. For instance, I wasn't any good at playing baseball. When my friends chose up sides for a ball game, I was always the last one to get picked.

I wasn't any good at hide-and-go-seek. When I closed my eyes to count to one hundred, I think my friends just went home.

Playing tag wasn't any better for me. When I was tagged and was *it*, I stayed *it*, and as far as I know, I'm still *it*.

When I got a little older and it came to girls, forget about it—I figured I was as interesting to girls as a fire hydrant. Across the hall from our apartment lived Mary. Mary was the prettiest girl in the world. The problem was that Mary dated older boys who slicked their hair back and wore black leather jackets.

The only thing I was any good at was reading. I liked to read books, such as Ian Fleming's James Bond novels, techno thrillers, science fiction, the Hardy Boys books, and Sherlock Holmes detective stories.

In September 1963, everything changed for me. I started high school. I wanted to go to the nearby high school with the neighborhood kids, but my English teacher, Sister Elizabeth, had other ideas. She wanted me to attend Cardinal Spellman High School, a scholarship high school only kids with good grades could attend.

"At Spellman you'll get a better education," Sister Elizabeth said, "and you'll be better prepared for college." My future was cast!

When I started going to classes at Spellman, I met lots of kids like me— boys and girls who were smart and good at reading. Nobody cared that I stank at baseball, hide-and-go-seek, and tag.

I joined the Spellman marching band and learned to play the clarinet. Every day after school we had band practice. And at practice, I couldn't keep my eyes off a pretty blond freshman named Cathy who sat nearby and played the saxophone. When I looked at her, she smiled at me.

One afternoon after practice, Cathy and I walked out of the band room at the same time.

"The school dance is this Friday night," she said to me. "Wanna go to the dance with me?" Cathy asked.

"Okay." That was all I could say. I was astonished. Cathy wrote her address on a slip of paper and gave it to me. I looked at the address and noticed her street wasn't far from school.

"Can I walk you home?" I asked with my heart pounding.

"Sure."

Cathy and I happily chatted all the way to her house. And later that week, we went to the school dance!

A New Beginning

In the years before I started high school, I wasn't very good at . . . well, anything. For instance, I wasn't any good at playing baseball—when my friends chose up sides for a ball game, I was always the last one to get picked.

I wasn't any good at hide-and-go-seek. When I closed my eyes to count to one hundred, I think my friends just went home.

Playing tag wasn't any better for me, either. When I was tagged and was *it*, I stayed *it*, and as far as I know, I'm still *it*.

When I got a little older and it came to girls, forget about it—I figured I was as interesting to girls as a fire hydrant. Across the hall from our apartment lived Mary. Mary was the prettiest girl in the world. The problem was that Mary dated older boys who slicked their hair back and wore black leather jackets, something I could never pull off.

The only thing I was any good at was reading. I liked to read books, such as Ian Fleming's James Bond novels, techno thrillers, science fiction, the Hardy Boys books, and Sherlock Holmes detective stories.

In September 1963, everything changed for me. I started high school. I wanted to go to the nearby high school with the neighborhood kids, but my English teacher, Sister Elizabeth, had other ideas. She wanted me to attend Cardinal Spellman High School, a scholarship high school only kids with good grades could attend.

"At Spellman you'll get a better education," Sister Elizabeth said, "and you'll be better prepared for college." My future was cast!

When I started going to classes at Spellman, I met lots of kids like me—boys and girls who were smart and good at reading; nobody cared that I stank at baseball, hide-and-go-seek, and tag.

I joined the Spellman marching band and learned to play the clarinet. Every day after school we had band practice. And at practice, I couldn't keep my eyes off a pretty blond freshman named Cathy who sat nearby and played the saxophone. When I looked at her, she actually smiled at me.

One afternoon after practice, Cathy and I happened to walk out of the band room at the same time.

"The school dance is this Friday night," she said to me. "Wanna go to the dance with me?"

In my astonished state, all I could say was a meek "Okay." Cathy wrote her address on a slip of paper and gave it to me. I looked at the address and noticed her street wasn't far from school.

"Can I walk you home?" I asked with my heart pounding.

"Sure."

Cathy and I happily chatted all the way to her house. And later that week, we went to the school dance!

Name _____ Date _____

Use what you read in the passage to answer the questions.

1. What does the word **scholarship** mean?

_____

_____

2. Where did Mary live?

_____

_____

3. Why did everything change for the writer in September 1963?

_____

_____

4. Why did Sister Elizabeth think the writer should go to Spellman High School?

_____

_____

5. What clues tell you that the writer did not want to go to Spellman at first?

_____

_____

6. What did Cathy do when the writer looked at her?

_____

_____

7. What clue tells you that the writer was nervous asking Cathy if he could walk her home?

_____

_____

8. What clues help you conclude that going to Spellman was a good idea for the writer?

_____

_____

Historical Fiction

What is historical fiction?

Historical fiction stories take place in the past. Historical fiction stories have characters, settings, and events based on historical facts. The characters can be based on real people or made up. The dialogue is made up. But the information about the time period must be authentic, or factually accurate. The stories explore a conflict, or problem, that a character has with himself, with other characters, or with nature.

What is the purpose of historical fiction?

Historical fiction blends history and fiction into stories that could have actually happened. It adds a human element to history. Readers can learn about the time period: how people lived, what they owned, and even what they ate and wore. Readers can also see how people's problems and feelings have not changed much over time. In addition, historical fiction entertains us as we "escape" into adventures from the past.

Who tells the story in historical fiction?

Authors usually write historical fiction in one of two ways. In the first person point of view, one of the characters tells the story as it happens to him or her, using words such as *I*, *me*, *my*, *mine*, *we*, *us*, and *our*. In the third person point of view, a narrator tells the story and refers to the characters using words such as *he*, *him*, and *his*; *she*, *her*, and *hers*; and *their*. The narrator may also refer to the characters by name, for example, "Patrick was proud to be part of the journey."

How do you read historical fiction?

The title gives you a clue about an important time, place, character, or situation. As you read, note how the characters' lives are the same as and different from people's lives today. Note the main characters' thoughts, feelings, and actions. How do they change from the beginning of the story to the end? Ask yourself: *What moves this character to take action? What can I learn today from his or her struggles long ago?*

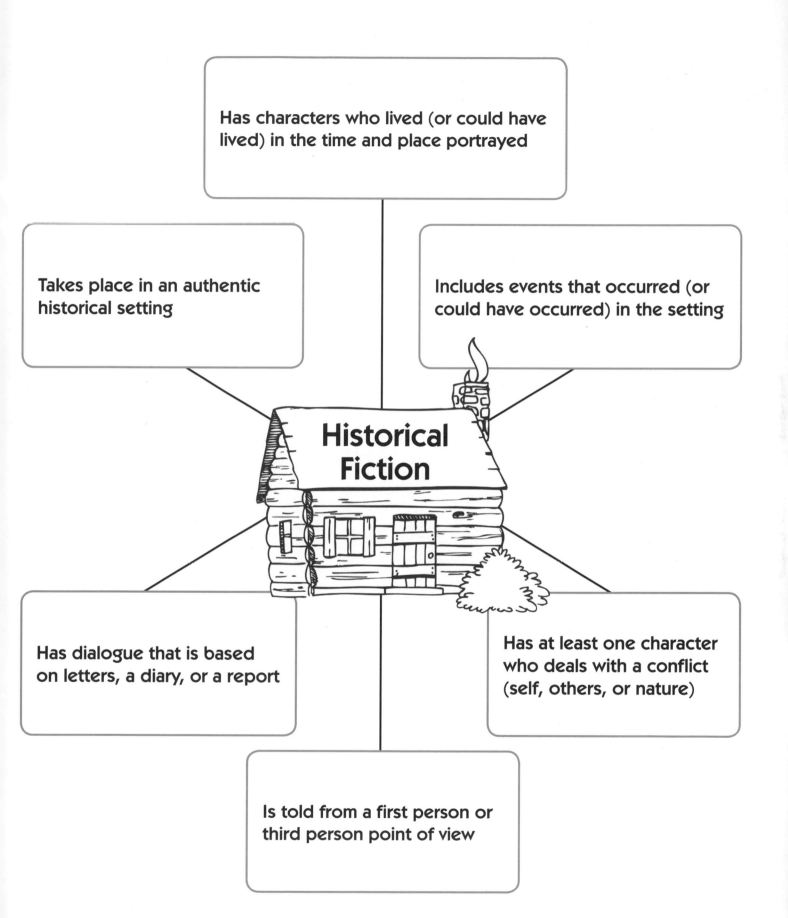

Has characters who lived (or could have lived) in the time and place portrayed

Takes place in an authentic historical setting

Includes events that occurred (or could have occurred) in the setting

Historical Fiction

Has dialogue that is based on letters, a diary, or a report

Has at least one character who deals with a conflict (self, others, or nature)

Is told from a first person or third person point of view

The Strong and the Weak: Hammurabi's Code

Ditanu was carving a plaque. He was following a pattern his master had created. His master was a stone carver. His name was Belshunu. Before now, Ditanu had been living with his uncle Lamusa. But Lamusa was a mean man. Belshunu offered to train Ditanu as a stone carver. He also offered Ditanu a home. Lamusa was happy to no longer worry about the boy.

One day a well-dressed woman walked angrily into the shop. "I am the Wife of Hudu-libbi," said the woman. "I want you to make me a votive figure of me," she told Belshunu. A votive figure is a small statue.

Only priests were allowed into temples where gods were worshipped. So wealthy people paid to have votives made. The votives looked like the person. That way the votives were inside the temple all the time. This way they could pray to the gods all the time.

"I'm busy with a royal job. It has King Hammurabi's laws carved into it. My apprentice Ditanu will make your votive."

The Wife of Hudu-libbi looked over at the young man. She said, "I'm going to stay and make sure this boy doesn't try to cheat me."

Ditanu rushed to finish the statue. He carefully made the size of the votive's nose smaller. Then he made lines and zigzags, which were the Wife of Hudu-libbi's jewelry. When he finished, the woman came over and looked at the votive figure very carefully.

"It looks almost entirely like me!" Before he could thank her, Ditanu heard a voice from the courtyard. It sent a shiver up his spine.

His dirty-looking uncle headed straight to Belshunu. "I've come to take my nephew," Lamusa said. "Come, dear nephew, and bring that pouch of silver with you."

"The boy stays here."

Everyone looked around. "Says who? Some nameless woman?"

"Law eighty-eight: 'If an artisan has undertaken to rear a child and teaches him his craft, the child cannot be demanded back.'" The Wife of Hudu-libbi continued in an angry voice, "You would break Hammurabi's laws and welcome the wrath of the gods?"

The god Shamash sat upright on a throne. He looked especially intimidating. Lamusa was afraid. He turned white under the gaze of the god. "I suppose you can keep the boy," he told Belshunu.

Lamusa turned and walked away. Thanks to the Wife of Hudu-libbi, Ditanu now knew that his home and bright future were both carved in stone.

The Strong and the Weak: Hammurabi's Code

Ditanu was carving a plaque. He was following a pattern his master had created. His master was a stone carver named Belshunu. Ditanu had been living with his uncle Lamusa. But Lamusa was a violent man. Belshunu had offered Ditanu an apprenticeship, or job, as well as a home. Lamusa was happy to no longer worry about the boy.

This morning Ditanu was perfectly happy. The future looked very bright.

A well-dressed woman stormed into the shop. "I am the Wife of Hudu-libbi," said the woman. "I want you to make me a votive figure of me," she told Belshunu. A votive figure is a small statue.

Only priests could go into temples where gods were worshipped. So wealthy people paid to have votives made in their likeness. This way they could pray constantly to the gods.

"I'm afraid I'm busy with a royal commission. It has King Hammurabi's laws carved into it. My apprentice Ditanu will make your votive."

The Wife of Hudu-libbi looked over at the young man. She said, "I'm going to stay and make sure this boy doesn't try to cheat me."

Ditanu rushed to finish the statue. He carefully made the size of the votive's nose smaller. Then he engraved lines and zigzags, which were the Wife of Hudu-libbi's jewelry. When he finished, the woman came over and looked at the votive figure very carefully.

"It looks almost entirely like me!" Before he could thank her, Ditanu heard a voice from the courtyard. It sent a shiver up his spine.

His dirty-looking uncle headed straight to Belshunu. "I've come to take my nephew off your hands," Lamusa said. "Come, dear nephew, and bring that pouch of silver with you."

"The boy stays here."

Everyone looked around. "Says who? Some nameless woman?"

"Law eighty-eight: 'If an artisan has undertaken to rear a child and teaches him his craft, the child cannot be demanded back.' " The Wife of Hudu-libbi continued in an angry voice, "You would break Hammurabi's laws and welcome the wrath of the gods?"

The god Shamash sat upright on a throne. He looked especially intimidating. Lamusa turned pale under the gaze of the god. "I suppose you can keep the boy," he told Belshunu.

Lamusa turned and skulked away. Thanks to the Wife of Hudu-libbi, Ditanu now knew that his home and bright future were both carved in stone.

The Strong and the Weak: Hammurabi's Code

Ditanu was carving a plaque, following a pattern his master had created. His master was Belshunu, a stone carver. Ditanu had been living in the home of his uncle Lamusa, a violent man. But Belshunu had offered Ditanu an apprenticeship, as well as a home. Lamusa was happy to no longer worry about the boy.

This morning Ditanu was perfectly happy. The future looked very bright.

A well-dressed woman stormed into the shop. "I am the Wife of Hudu-libbi," said the woman. "I want you to make a votive figure of me," she told Belshunu.

Only priests could go into the hearts of temples where gods were worshipped. So wealthy people commissioned statues called votives so they were able to pray constantly to the gods.

"I'm afraid I'm busy with a royal commission. It's inscribed with King Hammurabi's laws. My apprentice Ditanu will make your votive."

The Wife of Hudu-libbi looked over at the young man and said, "I'm going to stay and make sure this boy doesn't try to cheat me."

Ditanu rushed to finish the statue. He carefully reduced the size of the votive's nose. Then he engraved lines and zigzags representing the Wife of Hudu-libbi's jewelry. When he finished, the woman came over and scrutinized the votive figure.

"It looks almost entirely like me!" Before he could thank her, Ditanu heard a voice from the courtyard that sent a shiver up his spine.

His disheveled uncle headed straight to Belshunu. "I've come to take my nephew off your hands," Lamusa said. "Come, dear nephew, and bring that pouch of silver with you."

"The boy stays here."

Everyone looked around. "Says who? Some nameless woman?"

"Law eighty-eight: 'If an artisan has undertaken to rear a child and teaches him his craft, the child cannot be demanded back.'" The Wife of Hudu-libbi continued in thunderous tones, "You would break Hammurabi's laws and welcome the wrath of the gods?"

Shamash, who sat upright on a throne, looked especially intimidating. Lamusa turned pale under the gaze of the god. "I suppose you can keep the boy," he told Belshunu.

Lamusa turned and skulked off. Thanks to the Wife of Hudu-libbi, Ditanu now knew that his home and bright future were both carved in stone.

●●●

Name _____ Date _____

Use what you read in the passage to answer the questions.

1. What had Belshunu offered Ditanu?

_____

_____

2. What is Belshunu training Ditanu to be?

_____

_____

3. Why did the future look bright for Ditanu?

_____

_____

4. What clues let you infer that Ditanu was happy not to live with Lamusa?

_____

_____

5. What is the name of the woman who comes in the shop?

_____

_____

6. What is a votive figure?

_____

_____

7. Why did people have votive figures made?

_____

_____

8. What does the idiom "carved in stone" mean at the end of the passage?

_____

_____

The Day the Towers Fell

"Ninety-nine point six degrees," Mom said, reading the thermometer she'd just pulled out of my mouth. "Your fever is down but not gone."

She'd missed work yesterday to stay with me; she couldn't afford to miss another day and had to leave soon so she wouldn't be late. She always took the subway from our apartment in Chelsea to her receptionist job in the Financial District.

Today was September 11, 2001: a perfect sunny day to stay home from school. I found the remote, flopped onto the sofa, and turned on the television. There was some movie on about a burning skyscraper. Except it looked like it might be a news program. I went back to check.

The World Trade Center. Where my mom was. "Two commercial airliners have flown into the Twin Towers," the newscaster was saying. I ran to my bedroom and looked out the window. It was real. Mom's office was on the thirty-first floor of the North Tower.

Outside, the top of the South Tower—the part above the burning gash—tilted slightly, drooping. Then it dropped. In one long and terrible moment, the building collapsed downward, each floor gobbling the one beneath it.

I raced to the ringing phone in the kitchen. I pounced on the phone. "Mom? Hello? Mom?"

"Aaron?" It was Mom. I sagged with relief.

"Are you all right?" she asked.

"I'm fine. Are you all right? Where are you?"

"I'm in the lobby of a bank. I'm okay. I'm on my way home."

I watched the North Tower fall. I learned that there had been four concurrent hijackings; a third airplane had crashed into the Pentagon, and a fourth went down in a field in Pennsylvania. When my mom finally made it home, she was exhausted, bedraggled, and covered in white dust. Her hands and knees were bandaged. She cried as I hugged her.

"I never made it to work today. I was two blocks away when the North Tower was hit," she said. "I heard a terrible roar, and everyone around me started screaming and running. I looked back to see a tidal wave of ash and dust and debris coming down the street. In the panic I tripped and fell, but I managed to get up and duck into the nearest doorway just as the debris cloud hit."

September 11, 2001, was the most horrendous day of my life, but also one of the most memorable.

The Day the Towers Fell

"Ninety-nine point six degrees," Mom said, reading the thermometer she'd just pulled out of my mouth. "Your fever is down but not completely gone."

She'd missed work yesterday to stay with me; she couldn't afford to miss another day and had to leave soon so she wouldn't be late. She always took the subway from our apartment in Chelsea to her receptionist job in the Financial District of New York City.

Today was September 11, 2001, and it started out as a perfect sunny day to stay home from school. I found the remote, flopped onto the sofa, and turned on the television. There was some movie on about a burning skyscraper, but as I watched, it began to look like it might be a news program. I tried channel after channel, but the same thing was being shown on each one.

It was the World Trade Center. My mom worked there. "Two commercial airliners have flown into the Twin Towers," the newscaster was saying. I ran to my bedroom and looked out the window. It was real. Mom's office was on the thirty-first floor of the North Tower.

Outside, the top of the South Tower—the part above the burning gash—tilted slightly, drooping. Then it dropped. In one long and terrible moment, the building collapsed downward, each floor gobbling the one beneath it.

I raced to the ringing phone in the kitchen and pounced on it. "Mom? Hello? Mom?"

"Aaron?" It was Mom. I collapsed down onto the kitchen floor with relief.

"Are you all right?" she asked.

"I'm fine. Are you all right? Where are you?"

"I'm in the lobby of a bank. I'm okay. I'm on my way home."

I watched the North Tower fall. I learned that there had been four concurrent hijackings; a third airplane had crashed into the Pentagon, and a fourth went down in a field in Pennsylvania. When my mom finally made it home, she was exhausted, bedraggled, and covered in white dust. Her hands and knees were bandaged. She cried as I hugged her.

"I never made it to work today. I was two blocks away when the North Tower was hit," she said. "I heard a terrible roar, and everyone around me started screaming and running. I looked back to see a tidal wave of ash and dust and debris coming down the street. In the panic I tripped and fell, but I managed to get up and duck into the nearest doorway just as the debris cloud hit."

And that is why September 11, 2001, was the most horrendous day of my life—and also one of the most memorable.

The Day the Towers Fell

"Ninety-nine point six degrees," Mom said, reading the thermometer she'd just pulled out of my mouth. "Your fever is down but not completely gone."

She'd missed work yesterday to stay with me; she couldn't afford to miss another day and had to leave almost immediately so she wouldn't be late. She always took the subway from our apartment in Chelsea to her receptionist job in the Financial District of New York City.

Today was September 11, 2001, and it started out as a gloriously sunny day to stay home from school. I found the remote, flopped onto the sofa, and turned on the television. There was some movie on about a burning skyscraper, but as I watched, it began to look more like one of those special news programs that interrupt a regularly scheduled show. I tried channel after channel, but the same program was being broadcasted on each one.

They were talking about the World Trade Center, which was where my mom worked. "Two commercial airliners have flown into the Twin Towers," the newscaster was saying. I ran to my bedroom and looked out the window. It was real, all right, and Mom's office was on the thirty-first floor of the North Tower.

Outside, the uppermost part of the South Tower—the part above the burning gash—tilted slightly, drooping toward the ground. Then it dropped. In one long and devastating moment, the building collapsed downward, each floor gobbling the one beneath it.

I raced to the ringing telephone in the kitchen and pounced on it. "Mom? Hello? Mom?"

"Aaron?" It was Mom. I collapsed onto the linoleum floor with relief.

"Are you all right?" she asked.

"I'm fine," I replied. "Are you all right? Where are you?"

"I'm in the lobby of a bank," Mom answered. "I'm okay. I'm on my way home."

As I watched the North Tower fall, I learned that there had been four concurrent hijackings—a third airplane had crashed into the Pentagon and a fourth went down in a field in Pennsylvania. When my mom finally made it home, she was exhausted, bedraggled, and covered in white dust. Her hands and knees were bandaged. She cried as I hugged her.

"I . . . I . . . I was two blocks away from my office when the North Tower was hit," she stuttered. "I heard a terrible roar, and everyone around me started screaming and running. I looked back to see a tidal wave of ash and dust and debris coming down the street. In the panic I tripped and fell, but I managed to get up and duck into the nearest doorway just as the debris cloud hit."

And that is why September 11, 2001, was the most horrendous day of my life—and also one of the most memorable.

Name _____ Date _____

Use what you read in the passage to answer the questions.

1. What date did these events occur?

_____

_____

2. Why does Aaron think at first that the burning building on TV is a movie and not real?

_____

_____

3. Where was Mom's office?

_____

_____

4. Why did Mom not make it to work that day?

_____

_____

5. What happened after the South Tower was drooping?

_____

_____

6. How did Aaron feel when he heard Mom's voice on the phone?

_____

_____

7. What building did the third plane hit?

_____

_____

8. What clues tell you that on September 11, people came together to help one another through a bad time?

_____

_____

Myths and Legends

What are myths and legends?

A myth is a traditional story from an ancient culture that explains natural occurrences, such as how the world began or why the world is the way it is. The main character is often a god, goddess, or hero with special powers. A legend is a story based on a famous figure, place, or event. Legends are usually based on historical events, but they are fictionalized.

What is the purpose of myths and legends?

Long ago, people relied on myths and legends to explain natural events, such as violent storms or how a mountain or ocean came to be. Both legends and myths tell inspiring or cautionary adventure stories about people, places, or events that were important to a culture. They feature heroes who are strong, brave, and honest; the listeners learn good values from the actions of these heroes.

How do you read myths and legends?

As you read a myth, think about how the event is explained. Look for a hero, fantastic creatures, or gods with extraordinary powers. Ask yourself: *What does the main character do? How do these actions help explain an event?*

Do not look for a factual retelling of events or realistic portrayals of characters when you read a legend. Instead, look for unusual details and extraordinary people or creatures. Ask yourself what parts of the legend might be true and what parts make the legend unbelievable.

Who invented myths and legends?

In ancient times, storytellers told myths and legends to answer questions about the world. Their listeners understood the heroes of these myths, who were like a large cast of characters in an ongoing series. They were heroes with human qualities similar to their own, but their superpowers meant that they could perform amazing deeds. As the centuries passed, these stories were told and retold and then written down. Today science has explained the events in myths, but readers still enjoy the exciting adventures of the heroic characters.

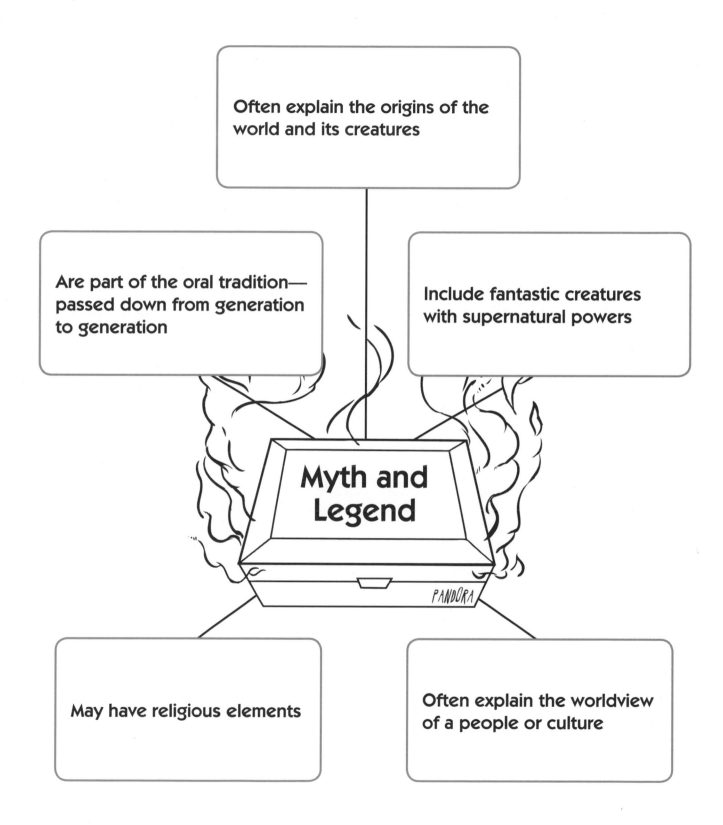

Often explain the origins of the world and its creatures

Are part of the oral tradition—passed down from generation to generation

Include fantastic creatures with supernatural powers

Myth and Legend

PANDORA

May have religious elements

Often explain the worldview of a people or culture

Ra Creates the World

Tell me what you see when your eyes are closed. Nothing, right? Before Ra created the world, that is all that existed. This nothingness had a name—Nun.

Nun groaned under its own weight. Inside Nun's heaviness there was force willing itself to life. This life was Ra. Ra burst through the black sea. Ra's loud voice shattered the quiet. He pushed and pushed until he had created a large mound, or hill. "I am Ra, the Shining One!" shouted the new force, or being, as he stood on top of the mound. He was glistening, or shining, brightly. That's because light was shining off of Ra. Before Ra, the nothingness was once dark. But the light of Ra now shone upon it.

Ra looked around with his one giant eye. He was not happy that there was only the mound. "I will create a great city!" he declared, and then created one. The city was beautiful, but there were no creatures. So Ra created all the animals and other living things of Earth. He named each one. "Here are sheep, and here are trees, and here are frogs," said Ra. He went on and on. He named all he had created. And Ra was pleased with what he now saw around him. But something was missing.

"I must have children," he said. "Children will bring me joy in my youth and care for me in my old age." Just as Ra had made himself come to life, his wish for children was so great that he brought up a giant sneeze from his soul.

"Shu!" exclaimed Ra as he sneezed, and suddenly Shu appeared. He was the god of air and the son of Ra. Ra adored Shu. But to have balance in this new world, he needed to create a female, or girl. Ra cupped his huge hands. He scooped up some of the water of Nun. He brought it to his lips and filled his mouth with the water. Then he spit out Tefnut. She was the goddess of moisture and rain.

Ra was very happy with all he had created. His greatest joy was being a father to Shu and Tefnut. One day, however, Shu and Tefnut went to play in the dark sea of Nun. Ra became worried when they hadn't returned for some time. His eye was able to come off of his face. So he sent his eye to look for his lost children. He replaced that eye with another one.

After Ra had waited nervously for some time, his first eye returned with the lost children. That eye saw the other eye on Ra's face. The first eye became very jealous. Ra took that jealous first eye and placed it on his forehead. There it could be in a position of special power to keep watch over the world.

Ra loved and enjoyed his children more than you could measure. He was **elated**, or filled with happiness. Tears of joy fell from his eyes, creating our ancestors.

Ra Creates the World

Tell me what you see when your eyes are closed. Nothing, right? Before Ra created the world, that is all that existed. This nothingness had a name—Nun.

Nun groaned under its own weight. Inside Nun's heaviness there was force willing itself to life. This life was Ra. Ra burst through the black sea. Ra's loud voice shattered the quiet. He pushed and pushed until he had created a large mound, or hill. "I am Ra, the Shining One!" shouted the new force, or being, as he stood on top of the mound. He was glistening, or shining, brightly. That's because light was shining off of Ra. Before Ra, the nothingness was once dark. But the light of Ra now shone upon it.

Ra looked around with his one giant eye. He was not happy that there was only the mound. "I will create a great city!" he declared, and then created one. The city was beautiful, but there were no creatures. So Ra created all the animals and other living things of Earth. He named each one. "Here are sheep, and here are trees, and here are frogs," said Ra. He went on and on. He named all he had created. And Ra was pleased with what he now saw around him. But something was missing.

"I must have children," he said. "Children will bring me joy in my youth and care for me in my old age." Just as Ra had made himself come to life, his wish for children was so great that he brought up a giant sneeze from his soul.

"Shu!" exclaimed Ra as he sneezed, and suddenly Shu appeared. He was the god of air and the son of Ra. Ra adored Shu. But to have balance in this new world, he needed to create a female, or girl. Ra cupped his huge hands. He scooped up some of the water of Nun. He brought it to his lips and filled his mouth with the water. Then he spit out Tefnut. She was the goddess of moisture and rain.

Ra was very happy with all he had created. His greatest joy was being a father to Shu and Tefnut. One day, however, Shu and Tefnut went to play in the dark sea of Nun. Ra became worried when they hadn't returned for some time. His eye was able to come off of his face. So he sent his eye to look for his lost children. He replaced that eye with another one.

After Ra had waited nervously for some time, his first eye returned with the lost children. That eye saw the other eye on Ra's face. The first eye became very jealous. Ra took that jealous first eye and placed it on his forehead. There it could be in a position of special power to keep watch over the world.

Ra loved and enjoyed his children more than you could measure. He was elated with happiness. Tears of joy fell from his eyes, creating our ancestors.

Ra Creates the World

Close your eyes and notice the nothingness. That is all that existed before Ra created the world. Unlike other nothingness, however, this one had a name—Nun.

The nothingness named Nun groaned under its own weight, but inside Nun's heaviness was a force willing itself into being—a force named Ra. Ra burst through the black sea and his piercing voice shattered the quietude. He pushed and pushed until he had created a large mound. "I am Ra, the Shining One!" shouted the newly emerged force as he stood on top of the mound. He was glistening brightly, for he radiated light; and where the nothingness was once dark, the light of Ra now shone upon it.

Ra looked around with his one giant eye, displeased that there was only the solitary mound. "I will create a great city!" he declared. So Ra created a magnificent city on top of the mound. The city was indeed beautiful, but it was devoid of creatures or other living things. So Ra created every animal and all vegetation on Earth and named them. "Here are fat cattle, and here are mighty oaks, and here are tiny frogs," said Ra. He went on and on, designating all he had created. Ra was pleased, though he felt something was still missing.

"I must have children," he exclaimed. "Children who will bring me joy in my youth and care for me in my old age." Ra's desire for children was so great that just as he had willed himself into being, he brought up a giant sneeze from his soul.

"Shu!" cried out Ra as he sneezed, and so appeared Shu, the god of air and the son of Ra. Ra delighted in Shu, but to have balance in this new world, it was essential to create a female. So Ra cupped his massive hands together, scooped up some of the water of Nun, brought it to his lips, and filled his mouth with the liquid. But rather than swallowing the water, he puffed up his cheeks and spit out Tefnut, the goddess of moisture and rain.

Ra was extremely satisfied with all he had created. His greatest satisfaction, however, was found in being a father to Shu and Tefnut. One fateful day, Shu and Tefnut wandered off to play in the dark sea of Nun. When they were gone for what Ra thought was an extraordinary amount of time, he became quite concerned. Ra had a removable eye that he could detach from his face, so he sent his eye to go look for his lost children. In the place of that eye, another appeared.

After Ra had waited anxiously for some time, his first eye returned with the lost children. The first eye saw the second eye on Ra's face and became fiercely jealous. Ra took the jealous first eye and placed it on his forehead, where it sat forever as a special watcher over the world.

Ra's joy at having his children back was immeasurable. He was so elated that happy tears fell from his eyes— and that is how he created our ancestors.

Name _____ Date _____

Use what you read in the passage to answer the questions.

1. Why does the author ask readers to close their eyes at the beginning?

_____

_____

2. Where did Ra come from?

_____

_____

3. What did Ra create on top of the mound?

_____

_____

4. What types of creatures did Ra create at first?

_____

_____

5. Why did Ra want children?

_____

_____

6. How did Ra create Shu?

_____

_____

7. What was Tefnut the goddess of?

_____

_____

8. What does the word **elated** mean?

_____

_____

Atlantis: Land of Sunken Dreams

Thousands of years ago there was a mighty Greek god named Poseidon. Poseidon ruled the sea, storms, and earthquakes. Poseidon was in love with a human woman. Her name was Cleito. He was so charmed by Cleito that he married her. Then he took her away to one of his islands. He had a fancy palace built especially for Cleito on top of a mountain. He created an entire nation for his bride. The people on the island were smart and **compassionate**, or kind. They were the type of people Poseidon wanted around Cleito to protect her.

Poseidon and Cleito had many children. Atlas was their oldest son. Atlas became the island nation's ruler. The island was known as the "Island of Atlas," or in Greek, "Atlantis."

The people of Atlantis, or Atlanteans, respected one another. They treated one another with kindness. There were no fights or crimes.

One day Atlas made a joke to the people. He said, "Perhaps we need a law that says we set aside one day each week for sorrow and suffering. That way, the people will appreciate our peaceful lives."

"But we don't have sorrow and suffering here," said the Atlanteans. "That's because we are better and smarter than everyone else. And we're more honest and work harder!"

"Interesting," Atlas said, with a hearty laugh. "It's true. We ARE better than the others, aren't we?"

Feeling a little too proud, the Atlanteans decided it was their job to tell other nations about how good they were. So they started to tell the rest of the world about their greatness. But they were very surprised by the reactions they got. They were not welcomed. Instead, they were treated as enemies. So the Atlanteans fought and conquered each nation they met.

Atlas was very angry at what had become of his people and his peaceful island nation. He thought of a way to fix things. The Atlanteans were getting ready for another battle when suddenly there was a very powerful explosion. It was more powerful than any on Earth before or since. Earth's crust cracked open at the center of the island. Clouds of ash and steam made the sky dark. The island started to disappear into the hole in Earth.

In just one day, Atlantis, with all its wealth and power, all its knowledge and artistry, all its history and ambition, disappeared into the sea. Atlantis was sunk by its own selfishness.

Atlantis: Land of Sunken Dreams

Thousands of years ago there was a mighty Greek god named Poseidon. Poseidon ruled the sea, storms, and earthquakes. Poseidon was completely in love with a human woman. Her name was Cleito. He was so enthralled, or charmed, by Cleito that he married her. Then he whisked her off to one of his islands. He had a fancy mountaintop palace built especially for Cleito. He created an entire nation for his bride. The people on the island were intelligent and considerate. They were compassionate. They were the kind of people Poseidon wanted to surround and protect Cleito.

Poseidon and Cleito had many children. Atlas was their oldest son. Atlas became the island nation's ruler. So the island came to be called the "island of Atlas," or "Atlantis" in Greek.

The people of Atlantis, or Atlanteans, respected one another. They treated one another with kindness. There were no fights or crimes.

One day Atlas made a joke to the people. He said, "Perhaps we need a law that says we set aside one day each week for sorrow and suffering. That way, the people will appreciate our peaceful lives."

"But we don't have sorrow and suffering here," said the Atlanteans. "That's because we are better, smarter, more honest, and work harder than everyone else!"

"Interesting," Atlas exclaimed, with a hearty laugh. "It's true, we are superior, or above others, aren't we?"

Feeling a little too smug, or proud, the Atlanteans decided it was their duty to tell other nations of their superiority. So the Atlanteans set out to tell the rest of the world the news of their greatness. But they were very surprised by the reactions they got. They were not welcomed for telling others about their perfection. Instead, they were treated as enemies. So the Atlanteans fought and conquered each nation they met.

Atlas was very angry at what had become of his people and his peaceful island nation. So he thought of a solution. The Atlanteans were preparing for another battle when suddenly there was a very power explosion. It was more powerful than any on Earth before or since. Earth's crust cracked open at the center of the island. Clouds of ash and steam made the sky dark. The island began to disappear into the hole in Earth.

In just one day, Atlantis, with all its wealth and power, all its knowledge and artistry, all its history and ambition, disappeared into the sea. Atlantis was sunk by its own selfishness.

Atlantis: Land of Sunken Dreams

Thousands of years ago, Poseidon was a mighty Greek god. He ruled the sea, storms, and earthquakes. Poseidon was enamored of, or in love with, a human woman named Cleito. He was so enthralled, or charmed, by Cleito that he married her. Then he whisked her off to one of his islands. He then had a lavish, or fancy, mountaintop palace built especially for Cleito. Poseidon created an entire nation for Cleito. The humans that inhabited, or lived on, the island were intelligent and compassionate, or kind. These were the type of people he wanted to surround and protect his bride.

Poseidon and Cleito had many children. Atlas was their oldest son. He became the island nation's ruler, and so it came to be called the "island of Atlas," or, in Greek, "Atlantis."

The people of Atlantis respected one another. They treated one another with kindness. There were no fights, crimes, or arguments of any kind.

"Perhaps we need a law saying Atlanteans should devote, or set aside, one day a week for sorrow and suffering," joked Atlas one day. "Perhaps our people will then appreciate our perfect existence."

"We don't have sorrow and suffering here," said the citizens of Atlantis. "That's because we are better, smarter, more honest, and more productive than everyone else!" Atlas exclaimed, with a hearty laugh. "It's true, we are above others."

That very day, the Atlanteans, feeling a little too smug, or proud, decided it was their moral obligation, or duty, to go out and tell other nations of their superiority.

So the Atlanteans set out to tell the rest of the world the news of their greatness. But to the great surprise of the Atlanteans, they were not welcomed for bringing their knowledge of paradise and perfection. Instead, they were treated as hostile invaders, or enemies. So the Atlanteans fought and conquered each nation they came across.

Atlas was outraged, or very angry at what had become of his people and his peaceful island nation. So he thought of a solution. As the Atlanteans prepared for another battle, an explosion more powerful than any on Earth before or since rocked the island nation. The crust of Earth cracked open at the center of the island. Clouds of ash and steam darkened the skies. The island began to disappear into the hole in Earth.

In just one day, the entire empire of Atlantis, with all its wealth and power, all its knowledge and artistry, all its history and ambition, disappeared into the sea. Atlantis was sunk by its own selfishness.

●●●

Name _____ Date _____

Use what you read in the passage to answer the questions.

1. Who was Poseidon?

_____

_____

2. What does the word **compassionate** mean?

_____

_____

3. Who became the ruler of the island nation?

_____

_____

4. What caused the Atlanteans to feel smug?

_____

_____

5. What effect did fighting with nations have on the Atlanteans?

_____

_____

6. What was Atlas's solution?

_____

_____

7. What happened to Atlantis?

_____

_____

8. What is the moral of this legend?

_____

_____

Science Fiction

What is science fiction?

Science fiction stories use scientific facts and technological developments to imagine a world that doesn't yet exist—but could. Sometimes the science is based on facts, and sometimes it is based on speculation. Often, the science and technology lead to a problem. Science fiction stories often take place in unusual settings, including outer space or distant futures.

What is the purpose of science fiction?

The purpose of science fiction is to reflect on how we live today by exploring imagined worlds. It sets out a possible (though sometimes highly improbable) situation and then explores it, usually in a serious way. Science fiction hopes to make readers think about the consequences today's actions may have for the future.

Who invented science fiction?

Some say that science fiction was invented when someone imagined an alternate world or life on another planet. In the early 1700s, Jonathan Swift wrote about a world with only tiny beings. In the early 1800s, Mary Shelley wrote about a scientist who brings a monster to life using body parts of dead people. More recent writers have explored the effect of computers and artificial intelligence on human beings and the universe.

How do you read science fiction?

Look for science and technology when you read science fiction. Ask yourself how these things are altering or changing the characters. Keep an open mind as you read. You are entering into a world of "what if." It might be a world of the future or the past. It might be on another planet or in another universe. It might even be a frightening world. But it is going to be an interesting trip.

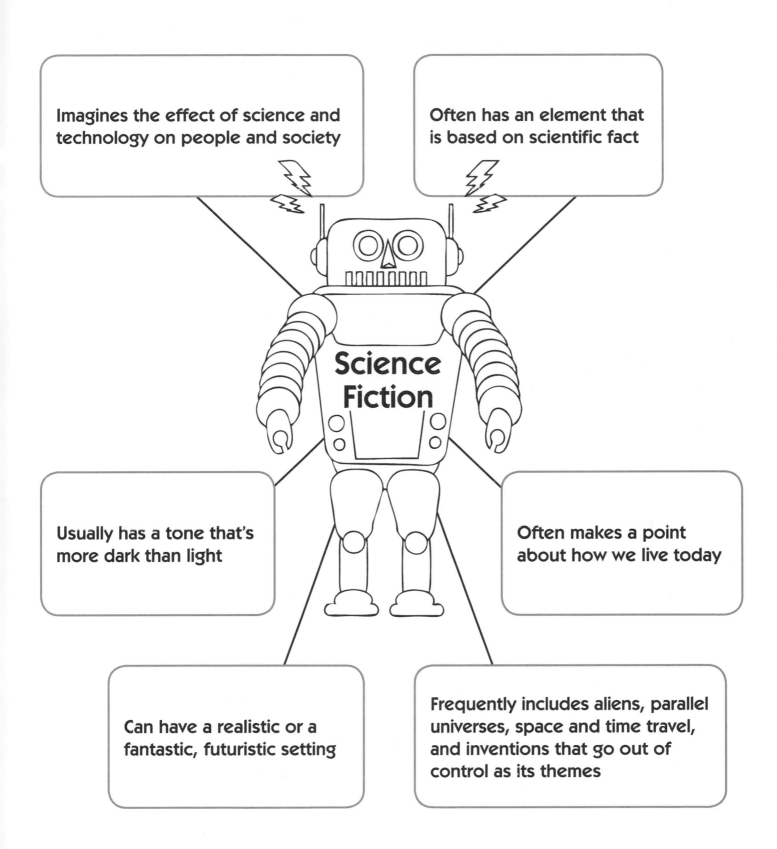

Imagines the effect of science and technology on people and society

Often has an element that is based on scientific fact

Science Fiction

Usually has a tone that's more dark than light

Often makes a point about how we live today

Can have a realistic or a fantastic, futuristic setting

Frequently includes aliens, parallel universes, space and time travel, and inventions that go out of control as its themes

Dream Pilot

Out in space dreams are very, very bad. I'm a pilot. I'm trained in everything from engine repair to navigation. But the biggest problem I face during star travel is loneliness. Starships travel very fast, faster even than the speed of light. The human brain isn't wired to handle that kind of speed. It drives most people crazy.

I'm different. When I was a cadet in the Interstellar Exploratory Fleet, doctors determined that with rigorous training my brain would be able to handle the nightmares of deep space. So I became a pilot. A pilot never, ever sleeps.

Nearing the halfway point between Earth and the faraway star of Tau Ceti, things are on schedule and going A-OK. Then, turning down the corridor, I spot a lurking monster. It's an enormous beast, bristling with spiky tufts of fur. It has nothing that looks like a head. Instead, a cluster of serpentine tentacles grows from its neck. The monster makes a sound like pudding being sucked from a boot.

I calmly approach the monster and walk past it. I don't give it a second glance. I know it will fade away as long as I pay no attention to it.

In the galley, I open the cabinet where the food processors are kept. Inside, a creature with long claws hangs upside down. Its red eyes are the size of grapefruits. Through its translucent skin, I can see branching blood vessels. I ignore this creature, too, and check the temperature meters on the processors.

The monsters and bulging eyes and tentacles and teeth are all just my waking nightmares. When ships go faster than the speed of light, space gets twisted and warped around them. The brain reacts with hideous nightmares.

I'm about to check on the water recyclers when the ship's alarm bells start screaming. I rush to the cockpit and activate the ship's sensors.

A four-engined ship looms in my view screen. The design is nothing like an Earth vessel. It is an alien ship.

A moment later, an incoming transmission arrives from the alien ship. I route it to my view screen. And a scream freezes in my throat. The creature has no head. Instead, tentacles extend from its neck. On the end of each tentacle snaps a mouth with sharp teeth. It's not alone. It's with the very same creature I saw in the food processor cabinet.

I know this monster. I saw it only several minutes before. It's the creature from the corridor. The one I ignored. The one I believed was only a nightmare. . . .

My nightmares aren't dreams. They're real. Or else, I've lost my mind to the empty reaches of deep space. I've gone mad! So I do the only sane thing I can think of. I arm the ship's missiles and place my hand on the launch button . . .

Dream Pilot

Out in space dreams are very, very bad. I'm a pilot and am trained in everything from engine repair to navigation. But the biggest problem I face during star travel is loneliness. Starships travel very fast—faster even than the speed of light. The human brain isn't wired to handle that kind of speed, and it drives most people crazy.

I'm different. When I was a cadet in the Interstellar Exploratory Fleet, doctors determined that with rigorous training my brain would be able to handle the nightmares of deep space. So I became a pilot because a pilot never, ever sleeps.

Nearing the halfway point between Earth and the faraway star of Tau Ceti, things are on schedule and going A-OK. Then, turning down the corridor, I spot a lurking monster. It's an enormous beast, bristling with spiky tufts of fur. It has nothing that looks like a head—instead, a cluster of serpentine tentacles grows from its neck. The monster makes a sound like pudding being sucked from a boot.

I calmly approach the monster and walk past it. I don't give it a second glance because I know it will fade away—as long as I pay no attention to it.

In the galley, I open the cabinet where the food processors are kept. Inside, a creature with long claws hangs upside down. Its red eyes are the size of grapefruits. Through its translucent skin, I can see branching blood vessels. I ignore this creature, too, and check the temperature meters on the processors.

The monsters and bulging eyes and tentacles and teeth are all just my waking nightmares. When ships go faster than the speed of light, space gets twisted and warped around them. The brain reacts with hideous nightmares.

I'm about to check on the water recyclers when the ship's alarm bells start screaming. I rush to the cockpit and activate the ship's sensors.

A four-engined ship looms in my view screen. The design is nothing like an Earth vessel. It is an alien ship.

A moment later, an incoming transmission arrives from the alien ship. I route it to my view screen, and a scream freezes in my throat. The creature has no head. Instead, tentacles extend from its neck. On the end of each tentacle snaps a mouth with sharp teeth. It's not alone. It's with the very same creature I saw in the food processor cabinet.

I know this monster—I saw it only several minutes before. It's the creature from the corridor, the one I ignored. The one I believed was only a nightmare. . . .

My nightmares aren't dreams. They're real. Or else I've lost my mind to the empty reaches of deep space. I've gone mad! So I do the only sane thing I can think of. I arm the ship's missiles and place my hand on the launch button . . .

Dream Pilot

Out in space dreams are very, very bad. I'm a pilot and am trained in everything from engine repair to navigation. But the biggest problem I face during star travel is loneliness. Starships travel very fast—faster even than the speed of light. The human brain isn't wired to handle that kind of speed, and it drives most people crazy.

I'm different. When I was a cadet in the Interstellar Exploratory Fleet, doctors determined that with rigorous training my brain would be able to handle the nightmares of deep space. So I became a pilot because a pilot never, ever sleeps.

Nearing the halfway point between Earth and the faraway star of Tau Ceti, things are on schedule and going A-OK. Then, turning down the corridor, I spot a lurking monster—an enormous beast, bristling with spiky tufts of fur. It has nothing that looks like a head—instead, a cluster of serpentine tentacles grows from its neck. The monster makes a sound like pudding being sucked from a boot.

I calmly approach the monster and walk past it. I don't give it a second glance because I know it will fade away—as long as I pay no attention to it.

In the galley, I open the cabinet where the food processors are kept. Inside, a creature with long claws hangs upside down, its grapefruit-sized red eyes glaring at me. Through its translucent skin, I can see branching blood vessels. I ignore this creature, too, and check the temperature meters on the processors.

The monsters, bulging eyes, long tentacles, and razor-edged teeth are all just parts of my waking nightmares. When ships go faster than the speed of light, space gets twisted and warped around them. The brain reacts with hideous nightmares.

I'm about to check on the water recyclers when the ship's alarm bells start screaming. I rush to the cockpit and activate the ship's sensors.

A four-engined ship looms in my view screen, but its design is nothing like an Earth vessel. It is an alien ship.

A moment later, an incoming transmission arrives from the alien ship. I route it to my view screen and a scream freezes in my throat. The creature has no head. Instead, tentacles extend from its neck; on the end of each tentacle a mouth with sharp teeth repeatedly snaps open and shut. And it's not alone—next to it is the very same creature I saw in the food processor cabinet.

I know this monster—I saw it only several minutes before. It's the creature from the corridor, the one I ignored. The one I believed was only a nightmare.

Are my nightmares dreams or are they really real? Or have I lost my mind to the empty reaches of deep space? I have to consider the possibility that I've gone mad. So I do the only sane thing I can think of—I arm the ship's missiles and place my hand on the launch button . . .

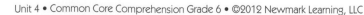

Name _____ Date _____

Use what you read in the passage to answer the questions.

1. What is the biggest problem with space travel?

_____

_____

2. Where was the narrator trained for this job?

_____

_____

3. This story took place in space, between Earth and . . .

_____

_____

4. What kind of creature does the narrator see first?

_____

_____

5. What did the monster have in place of a head?

_____

_____

6. What did the narrator compare the sound of the monster to?

_____

_____

7. Why did the narrator ignore the monster?

_____

_____

8. Why was the narrator scared at the end of the passage?

_____

_____

Varuna Takes a Job with the Census

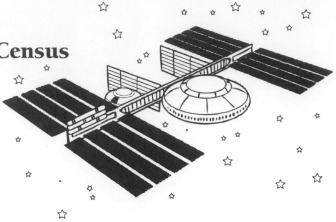

In a few moments, Varuna will be transported. She is going to UC, or Universe Central, for her first job. She'll be working for the Universal Census. The census is a count of all sentient beings in the universe. *Sentient* means conscious or living. The census happens once every ten billion years. It helps that Varuna is a Plynchin. As a Plynchin, she carries her own ecosystem. A Plynchin is a self-contained unit. Plynchins have extra-dimensional defenses. They use the defenses against any outside forces that might disrupt their breathing, food, and so on.

Varuna sees Universe Central as she beams in. It is amazing. The city is full of hubs and spokes and spires and wings. They stretch across the distance among a thousand stars. In fact, hundreds of stars are captured within force fields.

Suddenly Varuna finds herself in a smelly methane swamp. Methane is a gas. She is in her new boss's office. His name is Gphimpy. Gphimpy explains to Varuna that her job is to find every sentient being in Sector 689,142.021A-&.5. "Last time that was about eighty billion beings, so you'd better get going!" says Gphimpy.

Her first few assignments include several thousand planets. All of the planets have populations. During the last Census, however, this was not true. Back then, many of the planets in Varuna's sector had only some amino acids floating around in a soupy mass. With great delight, Varuna discovers dozens of new sentient populations!

Varuna has a very strange interview. The planet tells Varuna its history. During the last Census, ten billion years ago, this planet was just cooling from swirling gases. It was developing a crust and oceans back then.

"Then life began," says the planet. "The usual story." The planet tells Varuna about huge creatures. The planet can't remember how the giant creatures went extinct, or died out. It thinks maybe volcanoes killed the creatures, or maybe asteroid collisions.

Then the planet developed a life-form that was small but really smart. But this species competed and fought to take over the planet. Then it kept competing and fighting *with itself*.

"Oh, they destroyed their own habitat. They did a lousy job handling the changes that they made happen. For example, they heated up the planet and made a lot of things poisonous," explains the planet.

At the end of the day, Varuna beams home. She thinks how lucky she is that she isn't that lonely planet she met today. That single sentient being named Earth.

Varuna Takes a Job with the Census

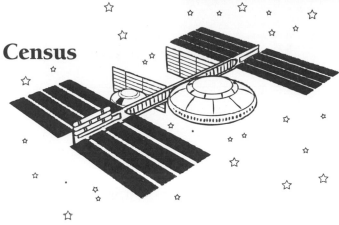

In a few moments, Varuna will be transported to UC, Universe Central. That's where she is going to take her first job. She'll be working for the Universal Census: a count of all sentient, or conscious, beings in the universe. The census happens once every ten billion years. It helps that Varuna is a Plynchin. As a Plynchin, she carries her own ecosystem. A Plynchin is a self-contained unit. Plynchins have extra-dimensional defenses against any outside forces that might disrupt their breathing, nourishment, and so on.

Varuna gets a view of the capital city of Universe Central as she beams in. It is spectacular. Its hubs and spokes and spires and wings stretch across the distance among a thousand stars. In fact, hundreds of stars are captured within force fields.

Suddenly Varuna finds herself in a smelly methane swamp. It is the office of Gphimpy, her new boss. Gphimpy explains to Varuna that her job is to find every sentient being in Sector 689,142.021A-&.5. "Last time that was about eighty billion beings, so you'd better get cracking!" adds Gphimpy.

Her first few assignments include several thousand planets. All of the planets have populations. At the time of the last Census, however, quite a few planets in Varuna's sector only had some amino acids floating around in a soupy mass. With great delight, Varuna discovers dozens of new sentient races, or populations!

Varuna has the strangest interview of the entire day. It's with a planet that tells Varuna its history. At the time of the last Census, ten billion years ago, this planet was just cooling from swirling gases. It was also getting a crust, developing oceans, and that sort of thing.

"Then life began," says the planet. "The usual story." The planet tells Varuna about huge creatures. The planet can't remember how those giant creatures went extinct, or died out. It thinks maybe volcanic eruptions, maybe an asteroid collision.

Then the planet developed a life-form that was small but really smart. Unfortunately, first this species competed and fought to take over the planet. Then it kept competing and fighting *with itself*.

"Oh, they destroyed their own habitat. They did a lousy job of reacting to the changes that they made happen, such as heating up the planet and making a lot of things that were poisonous," explains the planet.

At the end of the day, Varuna beams home. She thinks how lucky she is to not be that lonely planet she met today—that single sentient being named Earth.

Varuna Takes a Job with the Census

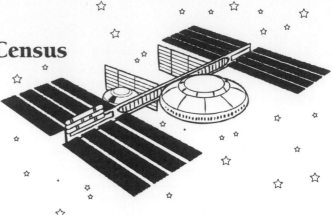

Varuna is moments away from being transported to UC, Universe Central. There she is going to take her first job, working for the Universal Census: a count of all sentient beings in the universe that happens once every ten billion years. Varuna, being a Plynchin, has a few advantages for this job. She carries her own ecosystem. A Plynchin is a self-contained unit with extra-dimensional defenses against any outside forces that might disrupt her breathing, nourishment, and so on.

Varuna gets a view of the capital city of Universe Central as she beams in. It is spectacular. Its hubs and spokes and spires and wings stretch across the distance among a thousand stars, and in fact hundreds of stars are captured within force fields.

Then Varuna finds herself in a smelly methane swamp, the office of Gphimpy, her new boss. Gphimpy explains to Varuna that her job is to find every sentient being in Sector 689,142.021A-&.5. "Last time that was about eighty billion beings, so you'd better get cracking!" adds Gphimpy.

Her first few assignments include several thousand planets with established populations. Quite a few planets in Varuna's sector, however, had only some amino acids floating around in a soupy mass at the time of the last Census. With great delight, Varuna discovers dozens of new sentient races!

The strangest interview all day happens with a planet that tells Varuna its history. At the time of the last Census, ten billion years ago, this planet was just cooling from swirling gases, getting a crust, developing oceans—that sort of thing.

"Then life began," says the planet. "The usual story." The planet tells Varuna about huge creatures. The planet can't remember how those giant life forms went extinct—maybe volcanic eruptions, maybe an asteroid collision.

Then the planet developed a lifeform that was small but really smart. Unfortunately, after this species had competed and fought to take over the planet, it kept competing and fighting *with itself*.

"Oh, they destroyed their own habitat. They did a lousy job of reacting to the changes they created by heating the place up and making a lot of things that were poisonous," explains the planet.

At the end of the day, Varuna beams home. She thinks how lucky she is to not be that lonely planet, that single sentient being named Earth, she met today.

Name _____ Date _____

Use what you read in the passage to answer the questions.

1. Where was Varuna's job?

_____

_____

2. How often does the Universal Census happen?

_____

_____

3. Why might it have been good that Varuna is a Plynchin?

_____

_____

4. What did the author mean by "beam in"?

_____

_____

5. Who was Gphimpy?

_____

_____

6. What were the giant life-forms that went extinct?

_____

_____

7. What caused them to go extinct?

_____

_____

8. Who were the small but smart life-forms the planet is telling Varuna about?

_____

_____

Overview II: Introduction to Informational Texts

What Is It?

What is an informational text?

Nonfiction text is an important tool for learning. Informational texts inform about social studies or science topics. Factual texts increase our knowledge of the world.

Examples

What are some examples of an informational text?

- Textbooks
- Encyclopedia Entries
- Reference Books
- Magazine Articles
- Brochures and Pamphlets
- Online Reference Articles

Purpose

What is the purpose of reading an informational text?

Informational texts help us learn information as well as expand our critical thinking skills by exposing us to different thoughts and issues. They also help prepare the brain for more difficult information as students continue schooling and prepare for real-life reading as an adult. Studies say reading informational texts can boost vocabulary and improve future reading and writing skills as well as attitudes about reading.

Audience

Who is the audience for an informational text?

Informational texts serve to educate the reader on a topic. Some readers prefer reading nonfiction to fiction. They would rather get information they can use or that makes them smarter than read imagined stories.

How to Use It

How do you read an informational text?

Before reading, have students think about what they already know about the topic. Then have them think about what they would like to know. Have students look for vocabulary words they do not know or that seem important, such as boldfaced or repeated words. Model and have children practice using reading strategies such as predict, monitor, inference, and summarize. After reading, follow up by asking students what they learned. Comprehension of informational texts is further aided by discussion and/or written response.

What are some common features of an informational text?

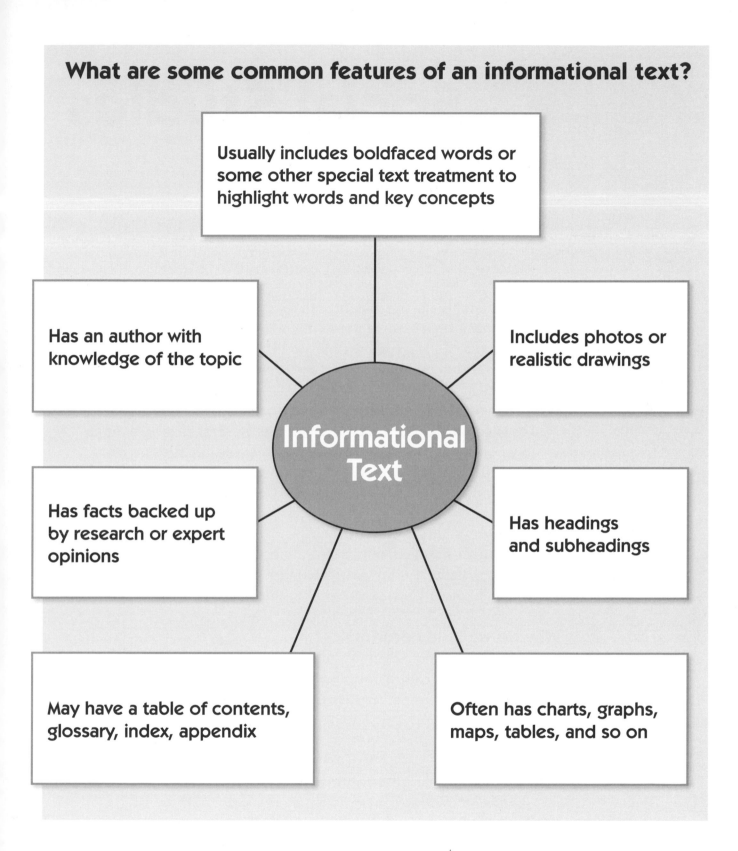

Usually includes boldfaced words or some other special text treatment to highlight words and key concepts

Has an author with knowledge of the topic

Includes photos or realistic drawings

Informational Text

Has facts backed up by research or expert opinions

Has headings and subheadings

May have a table of contents, glossary, index, appendix

Often has charts, graphs, maps, tables, and so on

Unit 5 Mini-Lesson
Social Studies

Why do we study social studies?

In social studies, people learn about the people in our world and how they relate to one another. We learn how they live, manage their communities, and relate to other groups. We also learn their values and what they seek to accomplish. We study the rights and responsibilities of people to one another. We learn the similarities and differences between people in different places or across different times. Learning these things helps give a person the intellectual skills he or she needs to be a functioning member of society and get along with a variety of people.

Why do we study ancient civilizations?

We examine the many people, places, and events that have led us to where we are today politically, philosophically, artistically, and scientifically. If we do not know from where we came, we have no map to take us where we should go next.

Why do we study geography?

The study of geography helps us understand the world we live in and its systems. We learn the similarities and differences between people in other lands so as to better understand our own land.

Why do we study economics?

Economics is more than just money. It is about running a business, running a government, and running your personal life. Economics studies the costs and benefits of a decision. As you get older, you will make economic decisions that will impact you, your family, and your country's economic conditions.

Why do we study government and citizenship?

Simply, an informed citizen is a better citizen. Our type of government requires participation and cooperation among citizens. We learn from the mistakes and successes in our own government and those of other governments. We then apply those learnings to future decisions and laws.

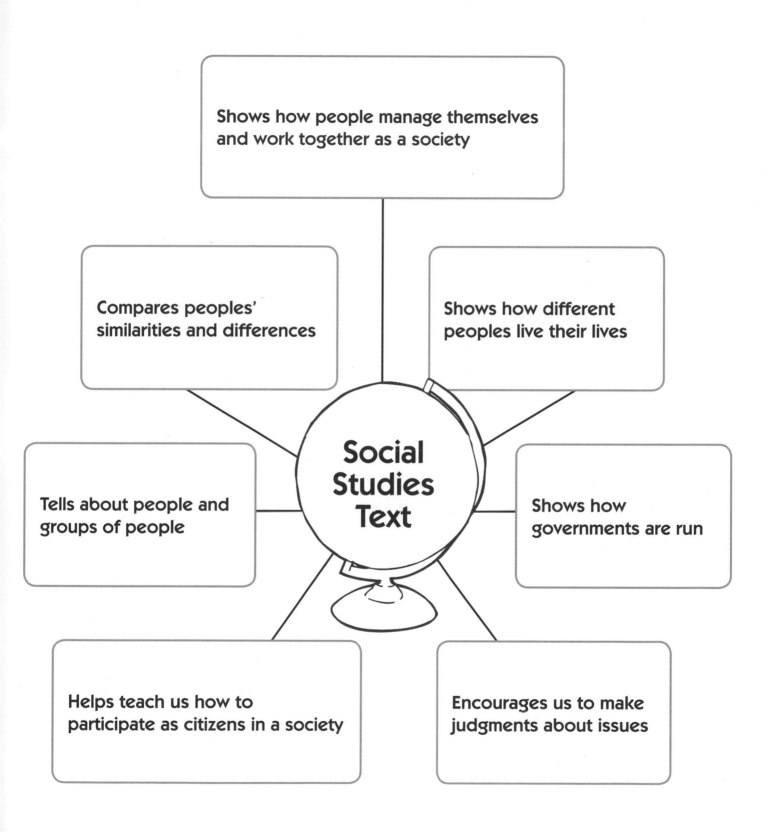

Shows how people manage themselves and work together as a society

Compares peoples' similarities and differences

Shows how different peoples live their lives

Social Studies Text

Tells about people and groups of people

Shows how governments are run

Helps teach us how to participate as citizens in a society

Encourages us to make judgments about issues

The Golden Age of Ancient Greece

The term *Golden Age* refers to a time when a culture or nation is at its greatest. The Golden Age in Athens was during the mid-400s B.C.E.

During the Golden Age, theater became very important. One type of play was a tragedy. Greek tragedies were usually about a person who faced a very difficult decision. Tragedies were part of a big festival held each year. The festival lasted for many days. Prizes were given for the best plays and the best acting. In Athens, there was an outdoor theater that had room for about 14,000 people. Greek plays are still performed today. Many of the ideas in these plays are still important.

Philosophy began in the Golden Age of Greece. The word comes from two Greek words meaning "love of wisdom." One of the most important Greek philosophers was Socrates. He explored a subject by asking people questions. These questions showed the weaknesses in someone's ideas.

Greek architects were also busy at work. They built many temples. The most famous temple was the Parthenon in Athens. The Parthenon was on the Acropolis. Greek sculptors created beautiful statues. They carved statues of gods, goddesses, and people. The statue of Zeus at Olympia was one of the Seven Wonders of the Ancient World.

The first known Olympic Games were held in 776 B.C.E. at Olympia in western Greece. After that, they were held every four years. In the first thirteen games, there was only one event—a running race of 192 meters (210 yards). Over the years, other events were added, such as wrestling, boxing, chariot racing, and horse racing. The Olympic Games were so important to the ancient Greeks that they even stopped wars for them. In 393 C.E., a Roman emperor ended the games. But warfare continued. This made the city-states weaker. At the same time, a country close to Greece was growing stronger.

The modern Olympic Games began in 1896.

●○○

The Golden Age of Ancient Greece

The term *Golden Age* refers to a time when a culture or nation is at its greatest. The Golden Age in Athens occurred during the mid-400s B.C.E.

During the Golden Age, theater became very important. One type of play was a tragedy, in which the main character faced a very difficult decision. Tragedies were part of an annual festival that lasted for many days. Prizes were awarded for the best plays and for the best acting. In Athens, there was an outdoor theater that had room for about 14,000 people. Greek plays are still performed today. They continue to use many of the ideas and situations from those plays because the ideas in them are still considered to be important.

The study of philosophy began in the Golden Age of Greece. The word comes from two Greek words meaning "love of wisdom." One of the most important Greek philosophers was Socrates. He explored a subject by asking people questions. The answers to these questions showed the weaknesses in people's ideas at the time.

Greek architects were also busy at work, building extravagant temples. The most famous temple was the Parthenon on the Acropolis in Athens. Greek sculptors created beautiful statues of gods, goddesses, and ordinary people. The statue of Zeus at Olympia later became one of the Seven Wonders of the Ancient World.

The first known Olympic Games were held in 776 B.C.E. at Olympia in western Greece. After that, they were held every four years. In the first thirteen games, there was only one event—a running race of 192 meters (210 yards). Over the years, other events were added, such as wrestling, boxing, chariot racing, and horse racing. The Olympic Games were so important to the ancient Greeks that they even stopped wars for them. In 393 C.E., a Roman emperor ended the games. But warfare continued, making the city-states weaker. At the same time, a country close to Greece was growing stronger.

The modern Olympic Games began in 1896.

The Golden Age of Ancient Greece

The term *Golden Age* refers to a time when a culture or nation is at its greatest. The Golden Age in Athens occurred during the mid-400s B.C.E.

During the Golden Age, theater became very important. One type of play was a tragedy, in which the main character faced a dreadfully difficult decision. Tragedies were part of an annual festival that continued for many days. Prizes were awarded for the best plays and for the best acting. In Athens, there was an outdoor theater that held an audience of about 14,000 people. Greek plays are still performed today. They continue to use many of the ideas and situations from those plays because the ideas in them are still considered to be important.

The study of philosophy began in the Golden Age of Greece. The word comes from two Greek words meaning "love of wisdom." One of the most important Greek philosophers was Socrates. Socrates explored a subject by asking people questions— the answers to these questions showed the weaknesses in people's ideas at the time.

Greek architects were also busy at work, building extravagant temples. The most famous temple, perhaps, is the Parthenon on the Acropolis in Athens. Greek sculptors created beautiful statues of gods, goddesses, and ordinary people. One such statue, the statue of Zeus at Olympia, later became one of the Seven Wonders of the Ancient World.

The first known Olympic Games were held in 776 B.C.E. at Olympia in western Greece. Subsequently, they were held every four years. In the first thirteen games, there was only one event—a running race of 192 meters (210 yards). Over the years, other events were added, such as wrestling, boxing, chariot racing, and horse racing. The Olympic Games were so important to the ancient Greeks that they even stopped wars for them. In 393 C.E., a Roman emperor ended the games; however warfare continued, making the city-states weaker. At the same time, a country close to Greece was growing stronger.

The modern Olympic Games began in 1896.

Name _____ Date _____

Use what you read in the passage to answer the questions.

1. What is a Golden Age?

_____

_____

2. When did the Golden Age in Athens begin?

_____

_____

3. What is a tragedy?

_____

_____

4. What clues let you know that theater was important to the ancient Greeks?

_____

_____

5. What is **philosophy** the study of?

_____

_____

6. What is the Parthenon?

_____

_____

7. What did great sculptors create for the Parthenon?

_____

_____

8. Name one of the seven wonders of the world mentioned in the passage.

_____

_____

Canada

Canada is the largest country in North America and the second-largest country in the world. Canada borders the Atlantic Ocean in the east. The Pacific Ocean forms the country's western border. To the north, Canada borders the Arctic Ocean.

Eastern Canada borders the Atlantic Ocean. Nova Scotia, Prince Edward Island, and New Brunswick are called the Maritime provinces. The Atlantic provinces used to be part of the Appalachian Mountains. Over time, the area wore down. Even so, many parts are rocky and hilly. The coastline has tall cliffs, inlets, and coves. Some places also have fjords. A fjord is a type of inlet. Inland, there are forests, farms, and swamps. Swamps are areas of wet, spongy ground.

The Saint Lawrence Lowlands make up much of the southern area of central Canada. A lowland is a region of low, flat land. The Saint Lawrence River flows through parts of the lowlands.

The southern area of central Canada borders the shores of four Great Lakes: Lake Ontario, Lake Erie, Lake Huron, and Lake Superior. The lakes were formed by melting glaciers. The water from Lake Ontario flows into the Saint Lawrence River.

The northern part of central Canada is part of the Canadian Shield. The Canadian Shield is a vast rock base. It is made up of some of Earth's oldest rocks. The shield lies under almost half of Canada. It has greatly affected the landscape of the country.

Western Canada includes wide-open prairies. Prairies are mostly flat, but they do have hills in some areas. The climate in the prairies is extreme. Winters are very cold and windy. Summers are very hot.

Forested wilderness stretches north of the prairies. Water covers almost one-sixth of this region. The biggest lake is Lake Winnipeg. It is 266 miles (428 kilometers) long.

The dry, grassy plains of the prairies gradually slope up to the west. They end about 2,000 feet (610 meters) above sea level. Then the Rocky Mountains rise abruptly above the plains. The Coast Range, covered in glaciers, lies still farther west. Between the two ranges are high, dry valleys.

Western coastal areas have Canada's wettest and mildest climate.

Much of far northern Canada is icy wilderness. Glaciers covered this land only 10,000 years ago. The area has the coldest temperatures and harshest landscape in Canada. It is called a tundra. Much of the north is too cold for trees.

Not all of the north is treeless and flat. Parts of the northwest are covered by huge mountains. Birch and spruce trees fill the large valleys.

Canada

Canada is the largest country in North America and the second-largest country in the world. Canada borders the Atlantic Ocean in the east. The Pacific Ocean forms the country's western border. To the north, Canada borders the Arctic Ocean.

Eastern Canada borders the Atlantic Ocean. Nova Scotia, Prince Edward Island, and New Brunswick are called the Maritime provinces. The Atlantic provinces used to be part of the Appalachian Mountains. Over time, the area wore down, but even so, many parts are rocky and hilly. The coastline has tall cliffs, inlets, and coves. Some places also have fjords, which are a type of inlet. Inland, there are forests, farms, and swamps, which are areas of wet, spongy ground.

The Saint Lawrence Lowlands make up much of the southern area of central Canada. A lowland is a region of low, flat land. The Saint Lawrence River flows through parts of the lowlands.

The southern area of central Canada borders the shores of four Great Lakes—Lake Ontario, Lake Erie, Lake Huron, and Lake Superior—which were all formed by melting glaciers. The water from Lake Ontario flows into the Saint Lawrence River.

The northern part of central Canada is part of the Canadian Shield, which is a vast rock base. It is made up of some of Earth's oldest rocks. The shield lies under almost half of Canada and has greatly affected the landscape of the country.

Western Canada includes wide-open prairies. Prairies are mostly flat, but they do have hills in some areas. The climate in the prairies is extreme. Winters are very cold and windy, and summers are very hot.

Forested wilderness stretches north of the prairies. Water covers almost one-sixth of this region. The biggest lake is Lake Winnipeg. It is 266 miles (428 kilometers) long.

The dry, grassy plains of the prairies gradually slope up to the west. They end about 2,000 feet (610 meters) above sea level. Then the Rocky Mountains rise abruptly above the plains. The Coast Range, covered in glaciers, lies still farther west. Between the two ranges are high, dry valleys.

Western coastal areas have Canada's wettest and mildest climate.

Much of far northern Canada is icy wilderness. Glaciers covered this land only 10,000 years ago. The area has the coldest temperatures and harshest landscape in Canada. Much of the north is tundra—too cold for trees.

Not all of the north is treeless and flat. Parts of the northwest are covered by huge mountains. Birch and spruce trees fill the large valleys.

Canada

Canada is the largest country in North America and the second-largest country in the world. Canada borders the Atlantic Ocean in the east. The Pacific Ocean forms the country's western border. To the north, Canada borders the Arctic Ocean.

Eastern Canada borders the Atlantic Ocean. Nova Scotia, Prince Edward Island, and New Brunswick are called the Maritime provinces. The Atlantic provinces used to be part of the Appalachian Mountains. Over time, the area wore down, but even so, many parts are rocky and hilly. The coastline has tall cliffs, inlets, and coves. Some places also have fjords, which is a type of inlet. Inland, there are forests, farms, and swamps, which are areas of wet, spongy ground.

The Saint Lawrence Lowlands make up much of the southern area of central Canada. A lowland is a region of low, flat land. The Saint Lawrence River flows through parts of the lowlands.

The southern area of central Canada borders the shores of four Great Lakes—Lake Ontario, Lake Erie, Lake Huron, and Lake Superior—which were all formed by melting glaciers. The water from Lake Ontario flows into the Saint Lawrence River.

The northern part of central Canada is part of the Canadian Shield, which is a vast rock base made up of some of Earth's oldest rocks. The shield lies under almost half of Canada and has greatly affected the landscape of the country.

Western Canada includes wide-open prairies that are mostly flat but have hills in some areas. The climate in the prairies is extreme, with winters being very cold and windy, and summers being very hot.

Forested wilderness stretches north of the prairies. Water covers almost one-sixth of this region. The biggest lake is Lake Winnipeg, which is 266 miles (428 kilometers) long.

The dry, grassy plains of the prairies gradually slope up to the west and end about 2,000 feet (610 meters) above sea level. Then the Rocky Mountains rise abruptly above the plains. The Coast Range, covered in glaciers, lies still farther west. Between the two ranges are high, dry valleys.

Western coastal areas have Canada's wettest and mildest climate.

Much of far northern Canada is icy wilderness. Glaciers covered this land only 10,000 years ago. This area has the coldest temperatures and harshest landscape in Canada, making it a tundra—too cold even for trees to grow.

Not all areas of the north are treeless and flat. Parts of the Canadian northwest are covered by huge mountains, and birch and spruce trees fill the large valleys.

●●●

Name _____ Date _____

Use what you read in the passage to answer the questions.

1. What is the largest country in North America?

_____

_____

2. Name the four "Great Lakes" that have a border in Canada.

_____

_____

3. Which oceans does Canada border?

_____

_____

4. What is the Canadian shield made of?

_____

_____

5. What are fjords?

_____

_____

6. What is a lowland?

_____

_____

7. Why might the most northern part of Canada be difficult to get to?

_____

_____

8. Why don't trees grow in the tundra?

_____

_____

Economics

Economics may not seem to have much to do with your life, but it does. Economics is the study of the choices people make about how to use their **resources**.

Economics is also about the production and **consumption**, or use, of goods and services. Production is what people make, or produce. Consumption is what people buy, or consume. Every day you make economic choices. You decide what products to buy or what services to use.

One set of choices people make is between needs and wants. Needs are the things we must have to live. Some basic human needs are food and water, shelter, and clothing. Without food, water, clothing, and a roof over your head, you would not survive very long.

Wants are all the things we enjoy having and doing. Perhaps your skateboard is your prized possession. You do not need your skateboard in order to survive. That is the difference between needs and wants.

Price plays an important role in all economic decisions. In most economies, price is affected by an important law of economics. This law is called the law of supply and demand. Supply is the amount of an item or service that is offered. Demand is your desire to buy the item or service combined with your ability to pay for it. The law of supply and demand works like this: If more people want a product than there is

product, the price goes up. If there is more product than people are asking for, the price goes down. An important idea in economics is scarcity, or shortage. An item or service is scarce when there is not enough for all the people that want it.

There are four basic types of economies in the world: traditional, command, market, and mixed.

In traditional economies, there is one system, or method of working. People in traditional economies often live in rural areas. They earn their living from hunting or farming.

In command economies, the government owns some or all of the main industries. In the most extreme command economies, the government owns almost all property as well.

Market economies are the most common. All business involves an agreement between the people who make things and the people who buy things. The law of supply and demand determines the price of things and how much people get paid for working in the market.

Mixed economies are generally market economies with some of the features of government control found in command economies. The United States and Canada are considered mixed economies.

Economics

Economics may not seem to have much to do with your life, but it does. Economics is the study of the choices people make about how to use their resources.

Economics is also about the production and consumption, or use, of goods and services. Production is what people make, or produce. Consumption is what people buy, or consume. Every day you make economic choices when you decide what products to buy or what services to use.

One set of choices people make is between needs and wants. Needs are the things we must have to live. Some basic human needs are food and water, shelter, and clothing. Without food, water, clothing, and a roof over your head, you would not survive very long.

Wants are all the things we enjoy having and doing. Perhaps your skateboard is your prized possession, but you do not need your skateboard in order to survive. That is the difference between needs and wants.

Price plays an important role in all economic decisions. In most economies, price is affected by an important law of economics. This law is called "the law of supply and demand." Supply is the amount of an item or service that is offered. Demand is your desire to buy the item or service combined with your ability to pay for it. The law of supply and demand works like this: If more people want a product than there is

product, the price goes up. If there is more product than people are asking for, the price goes down. An important idea in economics is scarcity, or shortage—an item or service is scarce when there is not enough for all the people that want it.

There are four basic types of economies in the world: traditional, command, market, and mixed economies.

In traditional economies, there is one system, or method of working. People in traditional economies often live in rural areas. They earn their living from hunting or farming.

In command economies, the government owns some or all of the main industries. In the most extreme command economies, the government owns almost all property as well.

Market economies are the most common type of economies. All business involves an agreement between the people who make things and the people who buy things. The law of supply and demand determines the price of things and how much people get paid for working in the market.

Mixed economies are generally market economies with some of the features of government control that are found in command economies. The United States and Canada are considered mixed economies.

Economics

Economics may not seem to have much to do with your life, but it does. Economics is the study of the choices people make about how to use their resources.

Economics is also about the production and consumption, or use, of goods and services. Production is what people make, or produce, and consumption is what people buy, or consume. Every day you make economic choices when you decide what products to buy or what services to use.

One set of choices people make is between needs and wants. Needs are the things we must have to live, such as food and water, shelter, and clothing. Without food, water, clothing, and a roof over your head, you would not survive very long.

Wants are all the things we enjoy having and doing. Perhaps your skateboard is your prized possession, but you do not need your skateboard in order to survive. That is the difference between needs and wants.

Price plays an important role in all economic decisions. In most economies, price is affected by an important law of economics called "the law of supply and demand." Supply is the amount of an item or service that is offered. Demand is your desire to buy the item or service combined with your ability to pay for it. The law of supply and demand works like this: If more people want a product than there is product, the price goes up. If there is more product than people are asking for, the price goes down. An important concept in economics is scarcity, or shortage—an item or service is scarce when there is not enough of it for all the people that want it.

There are four basic types of economies in the world: traditional economies, command economies, market economies, and mixed economies.

In traditional economies, there is one system, or method of working. People in traditional economies often live in rural areas and earn their living from hunting or farming.

In command economies, the government owns some or all of the main industries. In the most extreme command economies, the government owns almost all property as well.

Market economies are the most common type of economies. All business involves an agreement between the people who make things and the people who buy things. The law of supply and demand determines the price of things and how much people get paid for working in the market.

Mixed economies are generally market economies with some of the features of government control that are found in command economies. The United States and Canada are considered mixed economies.

Name _____ Date _____

Use what you read in the passage to answer the questions.

1. What does the word **resources** mean?

_____

_____

2. What are three human needs?

_____

_____

3. What is the difference between a need and a want?

_____

_____

4. What happens when the supply is greater than the demand?

_____

_____

5. If a country didn't have enough oil to meet demand, what would happen to the price of oil?

_____

_____

6. What is **consumption**?

_____

_____

7. How many types of economies are there?

_____

_____

8. In which type of economy does the government own some or all of the main industries?

_____

_____

Darfur

In a region called Darfur in the African country of Sudan, a violent conflict has killed thousands of people. The government of Sudan wants to stop a revolt by rebel groups. Civilian soldiers have attacked villages. The rebel soldiers want to kill or clear out the people who live there.

Conflicts between groups of people and nations are a part of life. But there are people working hard to bring peace and justice to countries around the world. They want to protect human rights. Human rights are basic rights such as the right to life and liberty, freedom of thought and expression, and equality before the law.

Sometimes it takes just one person to bring two sides together. Martti Ahtisaari works to bring peace between nations. Ahtisaari was born in Finland. The city he lived in was taken over by the Soviet Union. His experience gave him a "desire to advance peace and thus help others with similar experiences."

Ahtisaari spent fourteen years working for the United Nations. He helped bring peace to Namibia. Namibia is a country in Africa. The country was ruled by neighboring South Africa. Namibia wanted to rule itself. In 1990, thanks to the work of Ahtisaari, Namibia finally became an independent nation.

Many groups also work to bring peace to other parts of the world. The United Nations has sent peacekeepers to the world's worst war-torn regions since 1948. The U.N. now has eighteen different peacekeeping programs. There are more than 100,000 U.N. peacekeepers around the world.

Most U.N. peacekeepers are soldiers who help keep the peace. They do this by making sure that all parties to a treaty honor their promises. U.N. peacekeepers watch over cease-fires. They remove land mines, or buried explosives, that could harm citizens.

Other peacekeepers do the jobs that are necessary to build a lasting peace. Some are lawyers and economists. Others are doctors and aid workers. Some peacekeepers make sure that elections are safe and fair. Others train police officers and help set up new governments. Still others help refugees go back to their homes and rebuild their lives.

War is not the only cause of violence in the world. Some people take advantage of the poor and weak. The International Justice Mission (IJM) is an organization that fights slavery and other types of abuse.

In some countries, people are not allowed to vote. Those who try to vote can be threatened or killed. The International Foundation for Electoral Systems (IFES) works to make sure that people have a say in how their governments work.

Darfur

In a region called Darfur in the African country of Sudan, a violent conflict has killed thousands of people. The government of Sudan wants to stop a revolt by rebel groups. Civilian soldiers have attacked villages, killing and clearing out the people who live there.

Conflicts between groups of people and nations are a part of life. But there are people working hard to bring peace and justice to countries around the world and protect human rights. Human rights are basic rights such as the right to life and liberty, freedom of thought and expression, and equality before the law.

Sometimes it takes just one person to bring two sides together. Martti Ahtisaari works to bring peace between nations. Ahtisaari was born in Finland. The city he lived in was taken over by the Soviet Union. His experience gave him a "desire to advance peace and thus help others with similar experiences."

Ahtisaari spent fourteen years working for the United Nations. He helped bring peace to Namibia, a country in Africa. The country was ruled by neighboring South Africa. Namibia wanted to rule itself. In 1990, thanks to the work of Ahtisaari, Namibia finally became an independent nation.

Many groups also work to bring peace to other parts of the world. The United Nations has sent peacekeepers to the world's worst war-torn regions since 1948. The U.N. now has eighteen different peacekeeping programs. There are more than 100,000 U.N. peacekeepers throughout the world.

Most U.N. peacekeepers are soldiers who help keep the peace. They do this by making sure that all parties to a treaty honor their promises. U.N. peacekeepers monitor cease-fires. They remove land mines, or buried explosives, that could harm citizens.

Other peacekeepers do the jobs that are necessary to build a lasting peace. Some are lawyers and economists, others are doctors and aid workers. Some peacekeepers make sure that elections are safe and fair. Others train police officers and help set up new governments. Still others help refugees go back to their homes and rebuild their lives.

War is not the only cause of violence in the world. Some people take advantage of the poor and weak. The International Justice Mission (IJM) is an organization that fights slavery and other types of abuse.

In some countries, people are not allowed to vote. Those who try to vote can be threatened or killed. The International Foundation for Electoral Systems (IFES) works to make sure that people have a say in how their governments work.

 65

Darfur

In the African country of Sudan, in a region called Darfur, a violent conflict has killed thousands of people. The government of Sudan wants to stop a revolt by rebel groups. Militias attacked villages with the intent of killing or clearing out the residents.

Conflicts between groups of people and nations are a part of life. Fortunately, there are people working hard to bring peace and justice to countries around the world and to protect human rights. Human rights are basic rights such as the right to life and liberty, freedom of thought and expression, and equality before the law.

Sometimes it takes just one person to bring two sides together for peace. Martti Ahtisaari has dedicated his life to bringing peace between nations around the globe. Ahtisaari was born in a city in Finland. His city was later taken over by the Soviet Union. His experience gave him a "desire to advance peace and thus help others with similar experiences."

Ahtisaari spent fourteen years working for the United Nations to negotiate peace in Namibia, a country in Africa. The country was ruled by neighboring South Africa. Namibia wanted to rule itself. Finally, in 1990, thanks to the work of Ahtisaari, Namibia became an independent nation.

Many groups also work to bring peace to other parts of the world. Since 1948, the United Nations has sent peacekeepers to the world's worst war-torn regions. Today, the U.N. has eighteen different peacekeeping operations around the world. The U.N. has more than 100,000 peacekeepers.

Most U.N. peacekeepers are soldiers who help keep the peace by making sure that all parties to a treaty fulfill their promises. U.N. peacekeepers monitor cease-fires. They remove land mines, or buried explosives, that could harm citizens.

The other U.N. peacekeepers who are not soldiers perform the jobs that are necessary to build a lasting peace. Some are lawyers and economists, while others are doctors and aid workers. Some peacekeepers make sure that elections are safe and fair. Others train police officers and help set up new governments. Still others help refugees return to their homes and rebuild their lives.

War is not the only cause of violence in the world. Some people take advantage of the poor and weak. International Justice Mission (IJM) is an organization that fights slavery and other types of abuse.

In some countries, the citizens are not allowed to vote. People who try to vote can be threatened or killed. The International Foundation for Electoral Systems (IFES) works to make sure that citizens have a say in how their governments work.

Name _____ Date _____

Use what you read in the passage to answer the questions.

1. Where is Sudan?

_____

_____

2. Why are the people of Darfur fleeing their country?

_____

_____

3. What are examples of basic human rights?

_____

_____

4. Why has Martti Ahtisaari spent his life working toward peace?

_____

_____

5. What is the purpose of the United Nations?

_____

_____

6. What does the IJM fight?

_____

_____

7. Why might people in some countries be scared to vote?

_____

_____

8. Why is it important for all adult citizens of a country to be able to vote?

_____

_____

Unit 6 Mini-Lesson
Science

Why do we study science?

Science helps us understand the world around us. To participate in society, one must know some science. As examples, to cook dinner, you need to understand hot and cold, chemical reactions, and the effects of combinations of ingredients. To ride a roller coaster, you need to understand that centrifugal force will keep you in your seat. To choose not to smoke, you are choosing the health of your lungs over peer pressure. All of these decisions involve understanding science.

Why do we study life science?

Earth is full of life, and life science studies the living things on Earth. Life science studies animals and plants and the environments and habitats in which they live. Life science studies how living things meet their needs for water and food. It studies life cycles of living things—how they grow and change over time.

Why do we study environmental science?

Environmental science is the study of the environment we live in. It involves alternative energy systems, pollution control, natural resource management, and the effects of global climate change.

Why do we study physical science?

Physical science involves the study of nonliving things in our world. When you use a fan to cool yourself off, when you use a computer to send an e-mail, when you mix vinegar and water to clean windows, or when you use a magnet to pick up a tack, you are employing physical science. Physical science study in school often includes laboratory work, such as experiments.

Why do we study earth science?

Earth science is the study of the earth as well as things in outer space. Builders use earth science to protect their buildings against high winds and earthquakes. Fishermen use earth science to know the best times to fish, the best places for fishing, and which fish they should keep to be responsible stewards of the sea. Everyone needs to understand some earth science in order to be a caretaker of our planet.

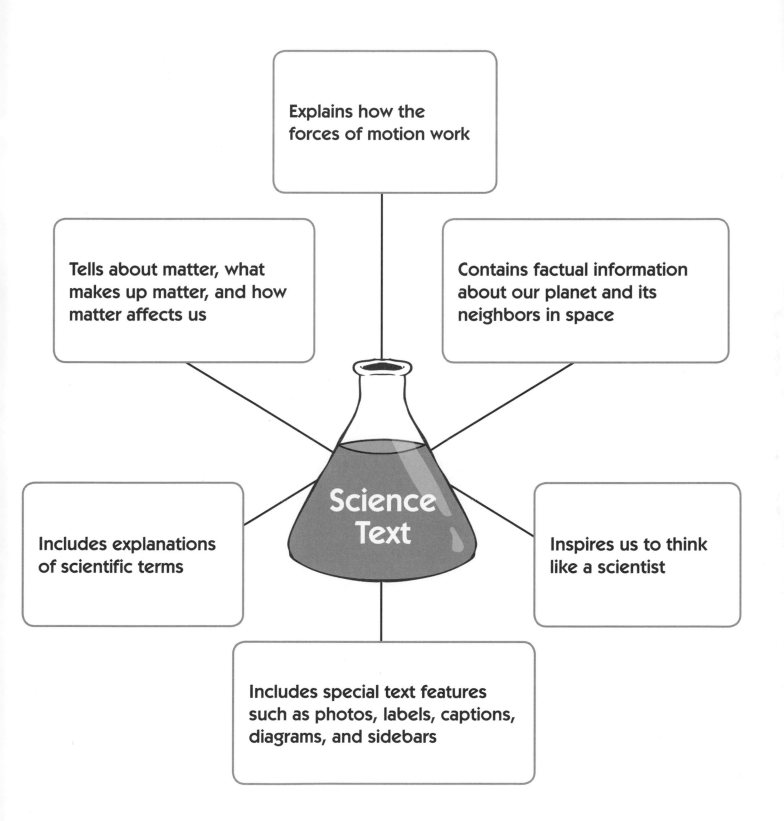

Explains how the forces of motion work

Tells about matter, what makes up matter, and how matter affects us

Contains factual information about our planet and its neighbors in space

Includes explanations of scientific terms

Science Text

Inspires us to think like a scientist

Includes special text features such as photos, labels, captions, diagrams, and sidebars

Living Together

There is a saying that "No man is an island." The saying means that none of us could survive alone. We all affect one another.

Communities of living things are also interconnected. The organisms may help one another survive. They also may compete with one another.

A milkweed plant growing along a country road interacts with many other community members. Caterpillars munch on milkweed leaves. **Fungi** grow on the roots of the milkweed. The fungi take in juices from the roots. In turn, the roots get water collected by the fungi from the soil. Members of two different species living in a close, nutritive relationship form a symbiosis.

The community also includes redtop grass. The roots and leaves of the redtop grass need the same sunlight, water, and nutrients as the milkweed plant. The two plants limit each other's growth. The milkweed plant is both helped and hindered by its neighbors.

Mutualism

Mutualism is a kind of symbiosis in which the relationship helps both living things. An example of a mutual relationship involves the human intestines. The intestines are full of bacteria sharing your food. The bacteria produce wastes. One of the waste products is vitamin K, which is an important vitamin for humans. Humans and the bacteria help each other.

Mutualisms help living things survive or reproduce. For example, honeybees get their food from flowers. The bees collect pollen and nectar to take back to their hive. The pollen on the bees' bodies is often carried from one flower to another. This helps the flowers create seeds. Without the bees, the plants could not reproduce. Without the flowers, the bees would starve.

Parasitism

Living things that feed off other living things and harm them are **parasites**. A parasite lives on or in the body of its host. When a leech fastens onto you and sucks your blood, you are its host. People can also host parasitic worms in their intestines, fungi on their feet, and viruses in their blood. Usually, parasites do not directly kill their hosts. Parasites usually weaken their hosts, making it harder for them to survive and reproduce.

●○○

Living Together

There is a saying that "No man is an island." The saying means that none of us could survive alone. We all affect one another.

Communities of living things are also interconnected. The organisms may help one another survive, but they also may compete with one another.

A milkweed plant growing along a country road interacts with many other community members. As an example, caterpillars munch on milkweed leaves. Fungi grow on the roots of the milkweed. The fungi take in juices from the roots. In turn, the roots get the water that was collected by the fungi from the soil. Members of two different species living in a close, nutritive relationship form a symbiosis.

The above-mentioned community also includes redtop grass. The roots and leaves of the redtop grass need the same sunlight, water, and nutrients as the milkweed plant. The two plants limit each other's growth. The milkweed plant is both helped and hindered by its neighbors.

Mutualism

Mutualism is a kind of symbiosis in which the relationship helps both living things. An example of a mutual relationship involves the human intestines. The intestines are full of bacteria sharing your food. The bacteria produce wastes, one of which is vitamin K, an important vitamin for humans. In this case, humans and bacteria help each other.

Mutualisms help living things survive or reproduce. For example, honeybees get their food from flowers. The bees collect pollen and nectar to take back to their hive. The pollen on the bees' bodies is often carried from one flower to another, which helps the flowers create seeds. Without the bees, the plants could not reproduce, and without the flowers, the bees would starve.

Parasitism

Living things that feed off other living things and harm them are parasites. A parasite lives on or in the body of its host. When a leech fastens onto you and sucks your blood, you are its host. People can also host parasitic worms in their intestines, fungi on their feet, and viruses in their blood. Usually, parasites do not directly kill their hosts. Parasites usually weaken their hosts, making it harder for them to survive and reproduce.

Living Together

The saying "No man is an island" means that none of us could survive alone—we all affect one another and are interconnected.

Communities of living things are also interconnected. The organisms in a community may help one another survive, but they also may compete with one another at the same time.

A milkweed plant growing along a country road interacts with many other community members. As an example, caterpillars munch on milkweed leaves. Fungi grow on the roots of the milkweed. The fungi take in juices from the roots. In turn, the roots get the water that was collected by the fungi from the soil. Members of two different species living in a close, nutritive relationship form a symbiosis.

The above-mentioned community also includes redtop grass, whose roots and leaves need the same sunlight, water, and nutrients as the milkweed plant. The two plants limit each other's growth. The milkweed plant is both helped and hindered by its neighbors.

Mutualism

Mutualism is a kind of symbiosis in which the relationship helps both living things. An example of a mutual relationship involves the human intestines. The intestines are full of bacteria sharing your food. The bacteria produce wastes, one of which is vitamin K, an important vitamin for humans. In this case, the humans and bacteria are helping each other.

Mutualisms help living things survive or reproduce. For example, honeybees get their food from flowers. The bees collect pollen and nectar to take back to their hive. The pollen on the bees' bodies is often carried from one flower to another, which helps the flowers create seeds. Without the bees, the plants could not reproduce, and without the flowers, the bees would starve.

Parasitism

Living things that feed off of other living things and harm them are called parasites. A parasite lives on or in the body of its host; for example, when a leech fastens onto you and sucks your blood, you are its host. People can also host parasitic worms in their intestines, fungi on their feet, and viruses in their blood. Usually, parasites do not directly kill their hosts, but weaken them, making it harder for them to survive and reproduce.

Name _____ Date _____

Use what you read in the passage to answer the questions.

1. Where do **fungi** grow?

_____

_____

2. How does fungi help a milkweed plant?

_____

_____

3. What do redtop grass and the milkweed plant compete for?

_____

_____

4. What is **mutualism**?

_____

_____

5. What happens after honeybees get nectar and pollen from flowers?

_____

_____

6. What are **parasites**?

_____

_____

7. Where do people get parasites?

_____

_____

8. What do parasites do to their hosts?

_____

_____

Deforestation

The buzz of a chain saw cuts through the quiet of a forest. Wood chips fly as the machine digs into the trunk of a very old tree. Suddenly, there's a loud creaking noise. A tree falls to the ground with a deafening crash. There are dozens of other fallen trees all around.

What was once part of the forest is now empty land. **Deforestation** happens when trees in an area are cut down and no new ones are planted. Deforestation is changing what land looks like all around the globe. Land is changing in other ways as well. In some places, areas that were once home to wild animals and plants lie dry and empty. The reason is desertification.

Over time, land that was once fertile has turned into desert. Sometimes nature is the cause. Other times, people are the reason.

What happens to forests? Why do they disappear? There are lots of reasons. Nature is often behind the forces that destroy forests. Wildfires happen when there is not enough rain. Forests dry out. Lightning strikes set off a blaze.

But forests are also destroyed by living creatures, both animals and humans. A termite's main source of food is wood. Every year, termites kill thousands of trees. Japanese beetles also pose a serious threat to trees. If unchecked, the pests can kill a tree by eating all the leaves or new growth.

Elephants rub against tree trunks to get rid of biting insects. In time, the tree bark wears away. The tree dies because it lost its protection. People are the biggest threat to forests. More people on Earth means a greater demand for food. Trees are often cut down or burned to prepare land for farming or ranching. In many countries throughout the world, people depend on wood for shelter, cooking, and heating.

Each year, thousands of trees are felled. Heavy equipment moves in to take the wood away. The earth gets packed down so hard that new growth is very difficult. Is your community getting bigger? Are trees being cut down to make way for homes, new roads, or a mall? That's what deforestation looks like.

About 8,000 years ago, more than half the land you know as the United States was forest. Today, less than one-quarter of the United States is forest.

Another major cause of deforestation is pollution. Pollution is the contamination of the environment. When toxic chemicals and waste materials get into the water and the soil, everything dies.

Deforestation

The buzz of a chain saw cuts through the quiet of a forest. Wood chips fly as the machine digs into the trunk of a very old tree. Suddenly, there's a loud creaking noise and a tree falls to the ground with a deafening crash. There are dozens of other fallen trees all around.

What was once part of the forest is now empty land. Deforestation happens when trees in an area are cut down and no new ones are planted. Deforestation is changing what land looks like all around the globe. Land is changing in other ways as well. In some places, areas that were once home to wild animals and plants lie dry and empty. The reason is desertification.

Over time, land that was once fertile has turned into desert. Sometimes nature is the cause, but other times, people are the reason.

What happens to forests and why do they disappear? There are lots of reasons. Nature is often behind the forces that destroy forests. When there is not enough rain, the forests dry out. Lightning strikes or careless campers are enough to set off a blaze, creating wildfires that burn hundreds of acres of forests and take days to extinguish.

But forests are destroyed by living creatures as well—both animals and humans. A termite's main source of food is wood. Every year, termites kill thousands of trees. Japanese beetles also pose a serious threat to trees. If unchecked, these pests can kill a tree by eating all the leaves or new growth.

Elephants rub against tree trunks to get rid of biting insects. In time, the tree bark wears away, causing it to die because it lost its protection. But people are the biggest threat to forests. More people on Earth means a greater demand for food. Trees are often cut down or burned to prepare land for farming or ranching. In many countries throughout the world, people depend on wood for shelter, cooking, and heating.

Each year, thousands of trees are felled. Heavy equipment moves in to take the wood away. The earth gets packed down so hard that new growth is very difficult. Is your community getting bigger? Are trees being cut down to make way for homes, new roads, or a mall? That is what deforestation looks like.

About 8,000 years ago, more than half the land you know as the United States was forest. Today, forested areas are less than one quarter of the United States.

Another major cause of deforestation is pollution, which is the contamination of the environment. When toxic chemicals and waste materials get into the water and the soil, everything dies.

Deforestation

The buzz of a chain saw cuts through the quiet of a forest. Wood chips fly as the machine digs into the trunk of a very old tree. Suddenly, there's a loud creaking noise and a tree falls to the ground with a deafening crash. There are dozens of other fallen trees all around.

What was once part of the forest is now empty land. Deforestation happens when trees in an area are cut down and no new ones are planted. Deforestation is changing what land looks like all around the globe, but land is changing in other ways as well. In some places, areas that were once home to wild animals and vegetation lie dry and empty. The explanation is the occurrence of desertification.

Over time, land that was once fertile has turned into desert. Sometimes nature is the cause, but other times, people are the reason.

What happens to forests and why do they disappear? There are a number of reasons. Nature is often behind the forces that destroy forests. For example, when there is not enough rain, forest material becomes dry and brittle. Lightning strikes or careless campers are enough to set off a blaze, creating wildfires that burn hundreds of acres of forests and take days to extinguish.

But forests are destroyed by living creatures as well—both animals and humans. A termite's main source of food is wood. Every year, these tiny creatures kill thousands of trees. Japanese beetles also pose a serious threat to trees. If unchecked, these pests can kill a tree by eating all its leaves and new growth.

Elephants rub against tree trunks to get rid of biting insects. In time, the tree bark wears away, causing it to die because it lost its protection. But people are the biggest threat to forests. More people on Earth means a greater demand for food, which in turn means that trees are often cut down or burned to prepare land for farming or ranching. And in many countries throughout the world, people depend on cut wood for shelter, cooking, and heating.

Each year, thousands of trees are felled and heavy equipment is sent in to take the wood away. The weight of the equipment causes the earth to get packed down so hard that new growth is very difficult. Is your community getting bigger? Are trees being cut down to make way for homes, new roads, or a mall? That is what deforestation looks like.

About 8,000 years ago, more than half the land we know as the United States was forest. Today, forested areas are less than one quarter of the United States.

Another major cause of deforestation is pollution, which is the contamination of the environment. When toxic chemicals and waste materials get into the water and the soil, living organisms die.

Name _____ Date _____

Use what you read in the passage to answer the questions.

1. What is **deforestation**?

_____

_____

2. How much of the United States is forest today?

_____

_____

3. What is making forests disappear?

_____

_____

4. How do forest fires happen? What happens first? Next?

_____

_____

5. What is one cause of deforestation?

_____

_____

6. What does the writer say deforestation looks like?

_____

_____

7. How much of the land was forest 8,000 years ago?

_____

_____

8. What is the definition of "pollution" in the article?

_____

_____

Forces

Softball is a game of forces and motion. A force is a push or a pull. Forces make things move. Forces also stop things from moving or change their direction. **Motion** is any change in an object's position.

It takes force to throw a ball. It takes force to hit a ball. And it takes force to stop a ball. Where do these forces—the pushes and pulls—come from? They start with your muscles. A lot of the muscles in your body are attached to bones. The muscles pull on the bones to move your body. Think of a softball pitcher here. The muscles in her shoulder pull on bones in her arm. This pulling lets her raise her arm back. Other muscles pull on bones to swing her arm forward. That swinging lets her give the ball a big push—a pitch. The ball flies toward home plate.

The pitcher uses force to start the ball moving. Now it's the batter's turn to use force. She holds the bat shoulder high. She steps forward and swings her arms across her waist. Dozens of muscles are pulling her bones. Then she hits the ball with the bat. *WHACK!* The bat changes the direction of the ball and gives the ball a big push. This force sends the ball high into the air.

The ball sails through the air. You know that it will fall back down. But that is only because the force of gravity pulls it down. Gravity is a force that pulls any two objects together. In this case, the two objects are Earth and the ball. Because Earth is so big, the pull of its gravity is strong. So no matter how high the ball is hit, it always comes back down.

Rubber balls aren't the only balls that bounce. When gravity pulls the softball down to the ground, it bounces a few times. Each bounce gets lower and lower. Then it rolls on the ground and stops.

Did the ball slow down and stop because it ran out of force? No, things don't run out of force. Rather, other forces acted on the ball to slow it down and stop it. One of those forces is friction. Friction arises when one surface rubs against another surface. Friction acts in a direction opposite to the motion of a moving object. Friction makes it harder for things to move. Each time a ball bounces, it rubs against the ground a little bit and slows down. When a ball rolls, it rubs against the ground a lot. The ball finally stops.

Meanwhile, the batter is racing down the first base line. She rounds the bag and heads for second. The outfielder picks up the ball and throws it to second base. The fielder throws the ball hard, but air resistance slows it down. Air resistance is friction between an object and gas particles in the air. The runner's hand reaches the base a split second before the ball. SAFE!

Forces

Softball is a game of forces and motion. A force is a push or a pull, and a force makes things move or stops things from moving, or changes their direction. Motion is any change in an object's position.

It takes force to throw a ball and to hit a ball; it takes force to stop a ball as well. Where do these forces—the pushes and pulls—come from? They start with the muscles in your body that are attached to bones. The muscles pull on the bones to move your body. Think of a softball pitcher, for example. The muscles in her shoulder pull on the bones in her arm and let her raise her arm back. Other muscles pull on bones to swing her arm forward, letting her give the ball a big push—a pitch. The ball flies toward home plate.

The pitcher has used force to start the ball moving. Now it's the batter's turn to use force. She holds the bat shoulder high, steps forward, and swings her arms across her waist. Dozens of muscles are pulling her bones. Then she hits the ball with the bat. *WHACK!* The bat changes the direction of the ball and gives the ball a big push, using force to send the ball high into the air.

The ball sails through the air, but you know that it will fall back down. That is only because the force of gravity pulls it down. Gravity is a force that pulls any two objects together—in this case, the two objects are Earth and the ball. Because Earth is so big, the pull of its gravity is strong, so no matter how high the ball is hit, it always comes back down.

When gravity pulls the softball down to the ground, it bounces a few times, but each bounce gets lower and lower. Then it rolls on the ground and stops.

Did the ball slow down and stop because it ran out of force? No, things don't run out of force. Rather, other forces acted on the ball to slow it down and stop it. One of those forces is friction, which is caused when one surface rubs against another surface. Friction acts in a direction opposite to the motion of a moving object, so it makes it harder for things to move. Each time a ball bounces, it rubs against the ground a little bit and slows down. When a ball rolls, it rubs against the ground around and around again, which means a lot of friction builds up and eventually causes the ball to stop rolling.

Meanwhile, the batter is racing down the first base line. She rounds the bag and heads for second. The outfielder picks up the ball and throws it to second base. The fielder throws the ball hard, but air resistance slows it down. Air resistance is friction between an object and gas particles in the air. The runner's hand reaches the base a split second before the ball. SAFE!

Forces

Softball is a game of forces and motion. A force is a push or a pull that makes things move, stops things from moving, or changes their direction. Motion is any change in an object's position.

It takes force to throw a ball and to hit a ball; it takes force to stop a ball as well. Where do these forces—the pushes and pulls—come from? They start with those muscles in your body that are attached to bones. The muscles pull on the bones to move your body. Think of a softball pitcher, for example. The muscles in her shoulder pull on the bones in her arm, allowing her to raise her arm and pull it back. Other muscles pull on bones to swing her arm forward, letting her give the ball a big push—a pitch. The ball flies toward home plate.

The pitcher has used force to start the ball moving. Now it's the batter's turn to use force. She holds the bat shoulder high, steps forward, and swings her arms across her waist; this is made possible by the dozens of muscles pulling on her bones. Then she hits the ball with the bat. The bat changes the direction of the ball and gives the ball a big push, using force to send the ball high into the air.

The ball sails through the air, but ultimately falls back down. That is because it is pulled down by the force of gravity, which is the force that pulls any two objects together—in this case, the two objects being Earth and the ball. Because Earth is so big, the pull of its gravity is strong—so no matter how high the ball is hit, it always comes back down.

When gravity pulls the softball down to the ground, it bounces a few times, but each bounce gets lower and lower. Then it rolls on the ground and stops.

Did the ball slow down and stop because it ran out of force? No, things don't run out of force, but rather, other forces act on each other—in this case, another force acted on the ball to slow it down and stop it. One of those forces is friction, which is caused when one surface rubs against another. Friction acts in a direction opposite to the motion of a moving object, making it harder for the object to move. Each time a ball bounces, it rubs against the ground a little bit and slows down. When a ball rolls, it rubs against the ground again and again, causing friction to build up and eventually causing the ball to stop rolling.

Meanwhile, the batter races down the first base line, rounds the bag, and heads for second. The outfielder picks up the ball and throws it to second base. The fielder throws the ball hard, but it is slowed down because of air resistance, which is friction between an object and gas particles in the air. The runner's hand reaches the base a split second before the ball. SAFE!

Name _____ Date _____

Use what you read in the passage to answer the questions.

1. What are two examples of forces?

_____

_____

2. What is **motion**?

_____

_____

3. How does a pitcher use force to throw a ball?

_____

_____

4. What does force allow a ballplayer to do?

_____

_____

5. How does a batter use the force of push to hit a ball?

_____

_____

6. What pulls a ball back to Earth?

_____

_____

7. Why does a rolling ball stop?

_____

_____

8. Air resistance is the friction between an object and _____?

_____

_____

What Is Energy?

Energy is one of the most basic features of the universe. Light, heat, sound, and electricity are all forms of energy. Energy is the ability to do work. Energy moves the cars down the street. Lamps need energy to make light. Trees need energy to grow. A lot of energy goes into building a city, as well.

Stored energy is called potential energy. Food, firewood, and gasoline all contain potential energy. Kinetic energy is energy of movement. It is the energy an object has because of the motion of its mass. Flowing water and blowing air have kinetic energy. A cyclist riding down a hill gains kinetic energy. As she increases her speed, her kinetic energy also increases. The faster something moves, the more kinetic energy it has. Energy can be converted from one form to another. Each time energy changes form, some of it turns into heat.

Energy Sources

Energy comes from many different sources. An energy source used to meet the needs of people is called an energy resource. You can think of an energy resource as the raw material from which energy is produced.

The sun is our most important source of energy. Sunlight, or solar energy, is a renewable resource that nature replaces in a short period of time. The energy of wind, waves, and running water also comes indirectly from solar energy.

Plants convert the kinetic energy of light into the potential energy of food. The food provides energy for growth and reproduction. Animals gain this energy when they eat the plants.

People use plant and animal materials, or biomass, as sources of energy, too. Some of the energy in the remains of ancient living things is preserved deep in the ground. Coal, natural gas, and petroleum are all found in the ground. These fuels are called nonrenewable resources because they cannot be replaced.

The heat inside Earth is an energy resource that does not come from the sun. Another nonsolar energy resource is nuclear energy. Nuclear energy is the potential energy stored in atoms.

What Is Energy?

Energy is one of the most basic features of the universe. Light, heat, sound, and electricity are all forms of energy. Energy is the ability to do work. Energy moves the cars down the street, lights the street lamps, and helps trees grow. A lot of energy goes into building a city as well.

Stored energy is called potential energy, and can be found in food, firewood, and gasoline. Kinetic energy is energy of movement. It is the energy an object has because of the motion of its mass. Flowing water and blowing air have kinetic energy, and so does a cyclist riding down a hill. As the cyclist increases her speed, her kinetic energy also increases, because the faster something moves, the more kinetic energy it has. Energy can be converted from one form to another. Each time energy changes form, some of it turns into heat.

Energy Sources

Energy comes from many different sources. An energy source used to meet the needs of people is called an energy resource. You can think of an energy resource as the raw material from which energy is produced.

The sun is our most important source of energy. Sunlight, or solar energy, is a renewable resource that nature replaces in a short period of time. The energy in wind, waves, and running water also comes indirectly from solar energy.

Plants convert the kinetic energy of light into the potential energy of food. The food in turn provides energy for growth and reproduction. Animals gain this energy when they eat the plants.

People use plant and animal materials, or biomass, as sources of energy, too. Some of the energy in the remains of ancient living things is preserved deep in the ground. Coal, natural gas, and petroleum are all found in the ground. These fuels are called nonrenewable resources because they cannot be replaced.

The heat inside Earth is an energy resource that does not come from the sun. Another nonsolar energy resource is nuclear energy, which is the potential energy that is stored in atoms.

What Is Energy?

Energy is one of the most basic properties of the universe. Light, heat, sound, and electricity are all forms of energy. Energy is the ability to do work—it moves automobiles down the street, lights the street lamps, and helps trees grow and blossom. A lot of energy is used in building and maintaining a city as well.

Stored energy is called potential energy, and can be found in food, firewood, and gasoline. Kinetic energy is energy of movement. It is the energy an object has because of the motion of its mass. Flowing water and blowing air have kinetic energy, and so does a cyclist riding down a hill. As the cyclist increases her speed, her kinetic energy also increases, because the faster something moves, the more kinetic energy it has. Energy can be converted from one form to another, although each time energy changes form, some of it turns into heat.

Energy Sources

Energy comes from a variety of sources. An energy source used to meet the needs of people is called an energy resource and can be thought of as the raw material from which energy is produced.

The sun is our most important source of energy. Sunlight, or solar energy, is a renewable resource that nature replaces within a short period of time. The energy contained in wind, waves, and running water also comes indirectly from solar energy.

Plants convert the kinetic energy of light into the potential energy of food. The food in turn provides energy for growth and reproduction. Animals gain this energy when they eat the plants.

People use plant and animal materials, or biomass, as sources of energy as well. Some of the energy in the remains of ancient living things is preserved deep in the ground. Coal, natural gas, and petroleum are all found in the ground; they are called nonrenewable resources because they cannot be replaced.

The heat inside Earth is an energy resource that does not come from the sun. An additional nonsolar energy resource is nuclear energy, which is the potential energy that is stored in atoms.

Name _____ Date _____

Use what you read in the passage to answer the questions.

1. What is **energy**?

_____

_____

2. What are two forms of energy?

_____

_____

3. How do trees use energy?

_____

_____

4. Food, wood, and gas have what kind of energy?

_____

_____

5. What is kinetic energy?

_____

_____

6. What sources of energy are found in the ground?

_____

_____

7. Name a form of energy that does not come from the ground or the sun.

_____

_____

8. What does the passage say is our most important source of energy?

_____

_____

Overview III: Introduction to
Opinions/Arguments

What Is It?

What is an argument?

An argument is a way of writing that tries to convince readers to believe or do something. An argument has a strong point of view about an idea or a problem. It includes facts and examples to support an opinion, and it usually suggests a solution.

Examples

What are some examples of an opinion/argument text?

- Essays
- Letters
- Editorials
- Speeches
- Advertisements
- Book and Film Reviews

Purpose

What is the purpose of an opinion/argument?

People write opinions and arguments to "sway," or change the minds of, their audience. They want readers to see their points of view. They may want readers to take action, too.

Audience

Who is the audience for an opinion/argument?

People write persuasive texts for all types of people: parents, friends, citizens, business leaders, world leaders, and others. They write letters, essays, and editorials to make people understand their views. A good persuasive writer knows his or her audience. He or she knows what facts and reasons might change the reader's mind.

How to Use It

How do you read an opinion/argument?

Keep in mind that the writer wants you to support his or her position. Ask yourself:

1. *What does the writer want or believe?*
2. *What is this writer's position, or opinion?*
3. *Does the writer support the argument/opinion with facts and good reasons?*
4. *Do I agree with the writer?*

What are some common features of an opinion/argument text?

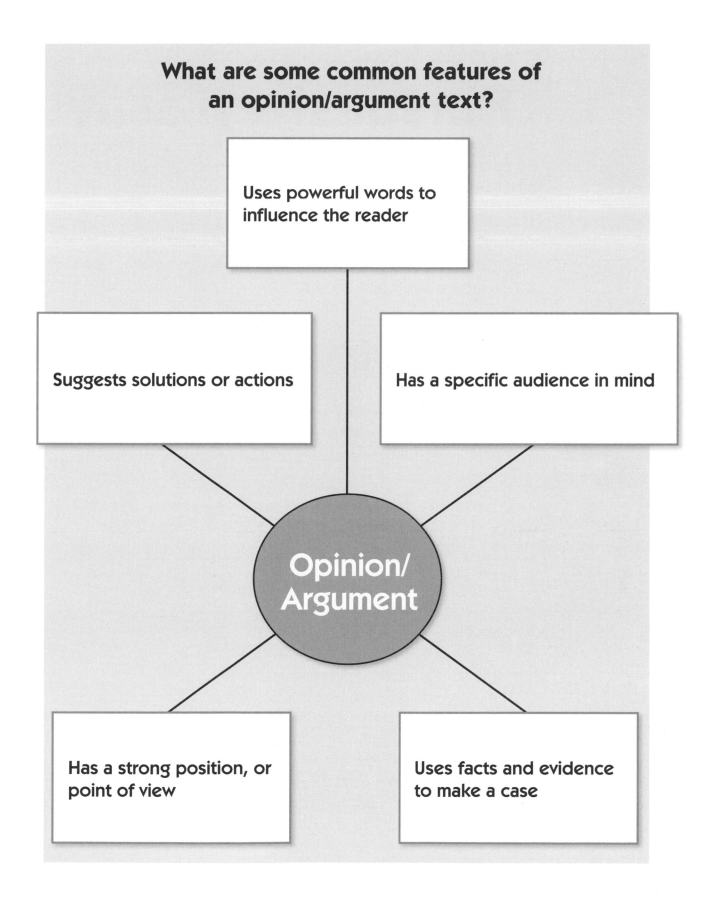

Uses powerful words to influence the reader

Suggests solutions or actions

Has a specific audience in mind

Opinion/Argument

Has a strong position, or point of view

Uses facts and evidence to make a case

Persuasive Essays

What is a persuasive essay?

A persuasive essay is an article that tries to convince the reader of something. It is typically short and to the point. It has a title, an introduction with thesis statement, supporting paragraphs, and a conclusion. The introduction catches the reader's attention with the topic and different opinions. Also in the introduction, the thesis states the problem to be presented and your solution. The supporting paragraphs summarize your opinions. It gives facts and examples. The conclusion grabs the reader with strong words about what the reader should do.

What is the purpose of a persuasive essay?

People write persuasive essays to hook their reader into a topic and then convince them your opinion is correct. The conclusion includes a "call to action." The reader must do something or believe something.

Who is the audience for a persuasive essay?

The audience for the essay depends on its purpose. Is it a letter to convince people that schools should start later? Then your audience might be people who can make that change. Is your article about the benefits of a later bedtime? Then your audience would be your parent or guardian.

How do you read a persuasive essay?

First determine what the writer wants to convince you to do or believe. Next see if the writer has made strong points in each supporting paragraph. The points should support his or her opinion. Look for facts in the article, such as expert opinions, references, or numbers. At the conclusion, decide whether you agree with the writer.

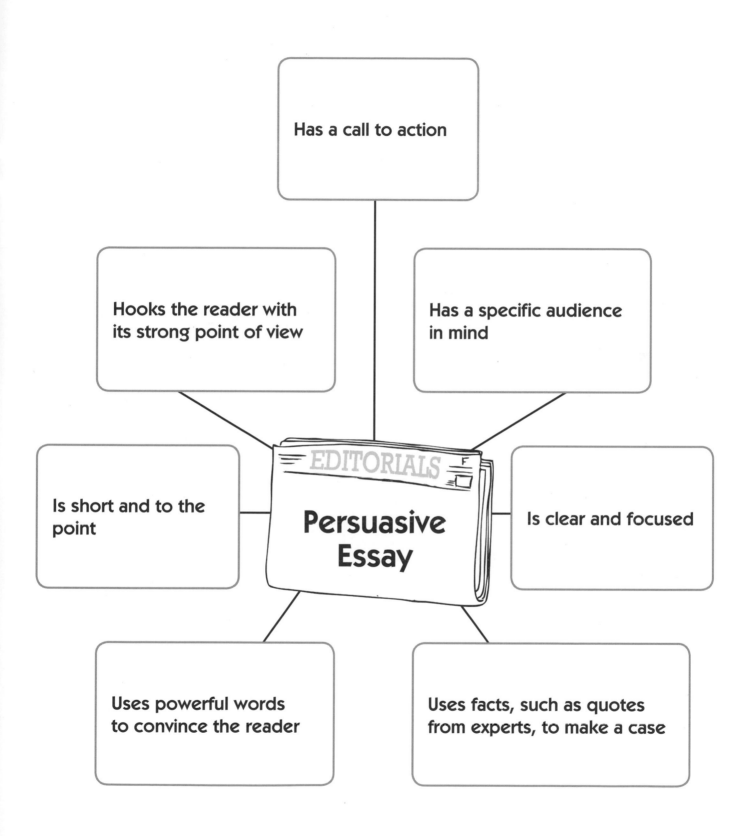

Has a call to action

Hooks the reader with its strong point of view

Has a specific audience in mind

Is short and to the point

Persuasive Essay

Is clear and focused

Uses powerful words to convince the reader

Uses facts, such as quotes from experts, to make a case

The Best Place to Live: Cities

City life is great. I love the lights. I love the sounds. I love the whirling crowds of people from around the world. To me, a city is the only place to live. City kids can have it all. There are places to run around, good schools, and so many fun things to do. Once you've lived in a city, you'll find living anywhere else **unfathomable**, or not possible to even think about. Of course, every city is a little different. Some cities are large and spread out, such as Los Angeles. People in cities like L.A. need to drive to get where they're going. Other cities, such as New York, are built in a more concentrated, or contained, area. Cities like New York have good public transportation, such as subways and buses.

Boston has something for everyone. Interested in sea animals? Check out the aquarium, or go on a whale watch. Do you like art? Spend the day at the Museum of Fine Arts or the Isabella Stewart Gardner Museum. If you like music, you can hear the Boston Symphony or the Pops. Or, if you are a musician, you can try out for the Youth Symphony. Sports fans in Boston can go see the Red Sox play at Fenway Park. Or watch a boat race on the Charles River. If you enjoy running, take a jog on the running paths along the river. Or you can watch the Boston Marathon, a 26.2-mile race in the city. In the winter, you can ice skate on Frog Pond. In warmer seasons, kids like me play soccer in any of the many parks.

Do you like great food? You can eat at Faneuil Hall, the North End, or Chinatown. Or have a picnic on the Boston Common. The Freedom Trail runs right past my school. On it you can see the Old North Church, Paul Revere's house, and more. What's the best part about Boston? You don't need your parents to drive you. You don't even need them to come along. Where else but in a city can kids enjoy this much freedom?

Cities have long been known as great melting pots. That means people from all different places and backgrounds coming together to live, learn, and work. This way of life has certainly had its share of problems, but it is also one of the best things about living in a city.

The Best Place to Live: Cities

City life. The lights. The sounds. The whirling crowds of people from so many cultures and places. For a kid who wants the most out of life, a city is the only place to live. City kids can have it all—places to run around, good schools, and plenty of fun things to do. Once you've sampled city living, you'll find the thought of living anywhere else unfathomable. Of course, every city is a little different from all the others. Some cities, such as Los Angeles, are large and sprawling. People generally drive from place to place. Other cities, such as New York, are built in a more concentrated area and have good public transportation (although people take taxis and drive cars, too).

In Boston, there's something for everyone. Interested in marine life? Check out the aquarium, or go on a whale watch. Art? Spend the day at the Museum of Fine Arts or the Isabella Stewart Gardner Museum. Like music? How about the Boston Symphony, the Pops?—or try out for the Youth Symphony and make your own music! Sports? Sit in the bleachers and watch the Red Sox play at Fenway Park. Or watch crew racing at the head of the Charles River. Come and watch (or, if you're at least eighteen, run in) the Boston Marathon. Anyone who likes running can use the running paths along the river. Or you could ice skate on Frog Pond in winter, play soccer in any of the many parks, or sail right down the Charles.

Do you like great food? Eat your way through Faneuil Hall, the North End, or Chinatown—or enjoy a picnic on the Boston Common. How about history? The Freedom Trail runs right past my school. What's the best part about all these activities? You don't need your parents to drive you, let alone come along. Where else but in a city can kids enjoy this much independence from their parents?

Cities have long been known as great melting pots, where people from all different places and socioeconomic backgrounds come together to live, learn, and work in a shared environment. While this way of life has certainly not been without problems, it can be one of the best things about living in a city.

The Best Place to Live: Cities

City life. The lights. The sounds. The whirling crowds of people from so many cultures and places. For a kid who wants the most out of life, a city is the only place to live. City kids can have it all—places to run around, good schools, and plenty of fun things to do. Once you've sampled city living, you'll find the thought of living anywhere else unfathomable. Of course, every city is a little different from all the others. Some cities, such as Los Angeles, are large and sprawling, so people generally drive from place to place. Other cities, such as New York, are built in a more concentrated area and have good public transportation (although people take taxis and drive cars, too).

In Boston, there's something for everyone. If you're interested in marine life, check out the aquarium, or go on a whale watch. If you're interested in art, spend the day at the Museum of Fine Arts or the Isabella Stewart Gardner Museum. And if you like music, you can go to the Boston Symphony, the Boston Pops, or try out for the Youth Symphony and make your own music! Are you a sports enthusiast? Sit in the bleachers and watch the Red Sox play at Fenway Park or watch crew racing at the head of the Charles River. Come and watch (or, if you're at least eighteen, run in) the Boston Marathon. Anyone who likes running can use the running paths along the river. Or you could ice skate on Frog Pond in winter, play soccer in any of the many parks, or sail right down the Charles.

Do you like great food? Eat your way through Faneuil Hall, the North End, or Chinatown—or enjoy a picnic on the Boston Common. How about history? The Freedom Trail runs right past my school. What's the best part about all these activities? You don't need your parents to drive you, let alone come along. Where else but in a city can kids enjoy this much independence from their parents?

Cities have long been known as great melting pots, where people from all different places and socioeconomic backgrounds come together to live, learn, and work in a shared environment. While this way of life has certainly not been without problems, it can be one of the best things about living in a city.

Name _____ Date _____

Use what you read in the passage to answer the questions.

1. Where does the writer think is the best place to live?

_____

_____

2. What does **unfathomable** mean?

_____

_____

3. How is Los Angeles different from New York City?

_____

_____

4. Where can you go in Boston if you want to hear music?

_____

_____

5. Where in Boston would you see a boat race?

_____

_____

6. What clues help you infer that the Freedom Trail is a historic walk in Boston?

_____

_____

7. Why does the writer know so much about Boston?

_____

_____

8. Why would you or wouldn't you want to live in Boston?

_____

_____

The Best Place to Live: Suburbs

Living in the **suburbs** is great. It is better than living in the city. It is better than living in the country, too. The suburbs are made for families. In the suburbs, there are always other kids around. The way suburbs are designed for families makes them the best place for a kid to grow up.

I live in Andover. It's a suburb twenty miles from Boston. Just over 30,000 people live in Andover. We have many kid-friendly activities. We also have movies, theaters, and ethnic restaurants, just like the city. Unlike the city, we don't have parking problems, long lines to get in places, and high prices. Like the country, suburbs have wide-open spaces to run around. But the playing fields are better and there are more of them.

In the suburbs, neighbors know each other. On my street, I know what every one of my neighbors looks like. They say hi to me and use my name. I have three friends who live within a quarter mile of my house. My mom and dad have a lot of friends, too. They help each other out, too. When our next-door neighbor had an operation, people in the neighborhood helped out. They took turns bringing dinner over. This way, his wife didn't have to worry about cooking.

The suburbs are great if you like sports. It doesn't matter if you are a star athlete or just want to get out and play ball. There's a state forest nearby, too. It has 3,000 acres of open space. We go there to fish, hike, bike, and ride horses.

Kids play sports in the country, the city, and the suburbs. But in the suburbs we have the space, rinks, fields, and pools for everyone to use. In the city, places to play sports are crowded. They are available only to organized teams that have money for expensive special permits.

In the country, people live far apart. It is not worthwhile for a town to build a place to play sports. In the country, people have to drive far to participate in organized sports.

People ask about the high cost of getting into the city from the suburbs. They also think we use our cars too much. My town has great public transportation into the city. We have both a bus and a train. It's true that we have to drive to stores. But since we have cars, we can buy in bulk, or large amounts. Then we don't need to go shopping as often. This saves a lot of energy over time.

If you enjoy peace and quiet and lots of insects, live in the country. If you're a kid who likes to run around, play sports, and hang out with lots of kids, the suburbs are the best. If you don't live in the suburbs, try to get your parents to move there!

The Best Place to Live: Suburbs

Living in the suburbs is much better than living in the city or in the country. The suburbs are very different from city and country living because they are built specifically for families. In the suburbs, kids are always around other kids. The suburb's family-centered design makes it the best place for a kid to grow up.

I live in Andover. It's a town twenty miles outside of Boston. Just over 30,000 people live here. The suburbs have plenty of kid-friendly activities, movies, theaters, and ethnic restaurants, just like the city. But unlike the city, we don't have to deal with parking problems, long lines to get in, and high prices. Suburbs also have wide-open spaces to run around in, just like the country. But the playing fields are better and more available.

Neighbors know each other in the suburbs. On my street, I know what every one of our neighbors looks like. They often greet me by name. I have three friends who live within a quarter mile of my house. My mom and dad have a lot of friends, too. We help each other out, too. When our next-door neighbor had an operation, people in the neighborhood took turns bringing dinner over. This way, his wife didn't have to worry about cooking.

There is something for every type of athlete, whether you are a star or just like to get out and play ball. There's a state forest nearby, too. It has 3,000 acres of open space for fishing, hiking, biking, and horseback riding.

Kids play sports no matter where you live. But in the suburbs we have the space, rinks, fields, and pools for everyone to use. In the city, places to play sports are crowded. As a result, the sports places are available only to organized teams that have money for expensive special permits.

In the country, people live far apart. So it is not worthwhile for a town to even build a place to play sports. In the country, people often have to drive far to participate in organized sports.

People ask about the high cost of commuting, or getting into the city. They also wonder about whether we use our cars too much. My town has great public transportation into the city. We have both a bus and a train. It's true that we have to drive to the grocery store and other stores. But the good thing is that since we have cars, we can buy in bulk, or large amounts, so we don't need to go shopping as often. This is a huge energy saver over time.

If you enjoy peace and quiet and swarms of insects, live in the country. If you're a kid who likes to run around, play sports, and hang out with lots of kids your own age, the suburbs can't be beat. If you don't live in the suburbs already, try to get your parents to move there!

The Best Place to Live: Suburbs

Living in the suburbs is way better than living in the city or out in the country. What really sets the suburbs apart from city and country living is that they were built specifically for families—so that kids could be around other kids. The suburb's family-centered design makes it the best place for a kid to grow up.

I live in Andover, a town that is twenty miles outside of Boston. There are just over 30,000 people here. Just like in the city, we have plenty of kid-friendly things to do, such as movies, theaters, and ethnic restaurants—but we don't have to deal with parking problems, long lines to get in, and high prices. And just like in the country, we have wide-open spaces to run around in. But the playing fields are in better shape and more available to everyone.

In my town, many people know their neighbors. On my street, we know what every one of our neighbors looks like. People often greet me by name. I have three friends who live close to my house. My mom and dad have a lot of friends, too. When our next-door neighbor had an operation, people in the neighborhood took turns bringing dinner over so his wife didn't have to worry about cooking.

Whether you're a star athlete or just like to get out there and play ball, the suburbs are where you want to live.

There's also a state forest nearby with 3,000 acres of open space for fishing, hiking, biking, and horseback riding.

Sure, kids play sports both in the city and in the country. But in the suburbs, we have enough space, rinks, fields, and pools for everyone to use. In the city, so many people want to use the sports facilities that they're often available only to organized teams that have money for special permits.

In the country, there aren't enough people living in one area to make it worthwhile for a town to even build those kinds of places. So people in the country often have to drive a long way to take part in organized sports.

Some people say, "But what about the high cost of commuting? What about having to use a car all the time?" It's true that we have to drive to the grocery store and other stores to do errands. But the upside is that we're able to buy in bulk and not go shopping as often. It's a huge energy saver in the long run.

If you're a kid who likes to run around, play sports, and hang out with lots of kids your own age, the suburbs can't be beat. If you don't live in the suburbs already, try to convince your parents to move there!

Name _____ Date _____

Use what you read in the passage to answer the questions.

1. What are **suburbs**?

_____

_____

2. In what way are suburbs made for families?

_____

_____

3. Where does the writer live?

_____

_____

4. What can you do for fun in the writer's town?

_____

_____

5. How many people live in the writer's town?

_____

_____

6. What clues help you infer that people in the suburbs are friendly?

_____

_____

7. Why is a suburb a better place to play sports than the city or the country?

_____

_____

8. Did the writer persuade you to prefer the suburbs? Tell why or why not.

_____

_____

Unit 8 Mini-Lesson
Book and Film Reviews

What are book and film reviews?

A book or film review is a summary of comments and opinions about a book or film. The writer tells what happens and shares his or her opinions about the book or film. The writer tells what is good about it and what might be bad or weak. The writer uses details from the book or film to support his or her opinions.

What is the purpose of book and film reviews?

Many people like to know about a book or film before they read or see it. That way they know if the book or film is a right match for them. Does the subject interest them? A book review helps the reader decide whether to read a book. A film review helps a person decide whether to see a movie.

Who is the audience for book and film reviews?

The audience for the book or film review depends on the audience for the book or film, as well as the audience where the review will be printed. The audience will be people interested in that subject. The reviewer writes to all of the people who might want to read the book or see the film that he or she is reviewing.

How do you read book and film reviews?

Pay attention to the plot, characters, and subject matter. Does the story line appeal to you? Did it interest the reviewer? How can you tell? Ask yourself: *What did the reviewer like? What did the reviewer dislike? Did he or she give good reasons for his or her opinions? Do I want to read the book or see the film now?*

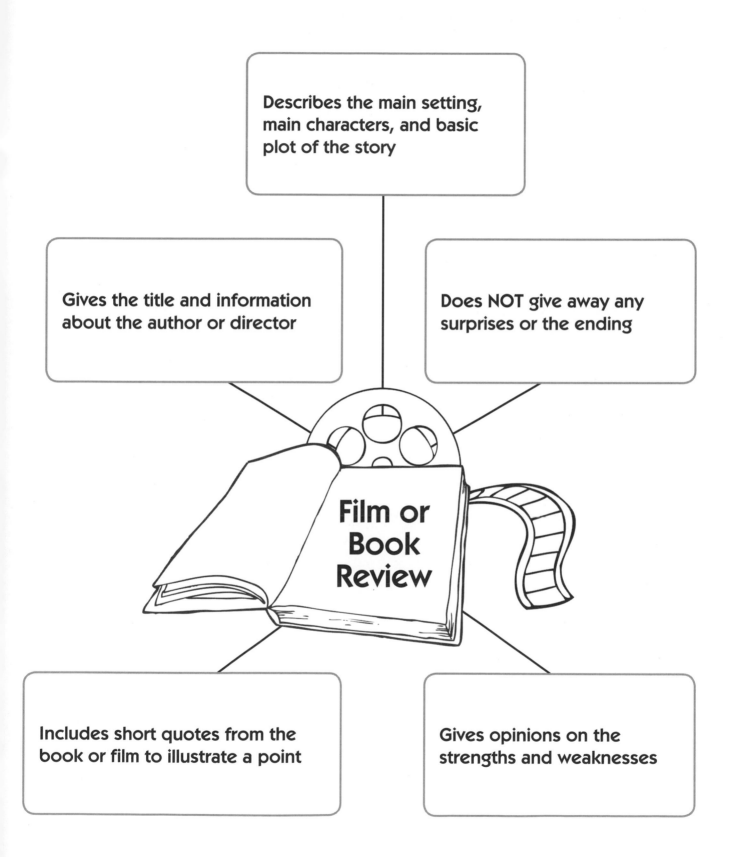

Describes the main setting, main characters, and basic plot of the story

Gives the title and information about the author or director

Does NOT give away any surprises or the ending

Film or Book Review

Includes short quotes from the book or film to illustrate a point

Gives opinions on the strengths and weaknesses

Matilda: Book Review

Matilda is a children's book by British author Roald Dahl. It was published in 1988. It's about an unhappy girl who is a genius. The problem is she is trapped in a rotten family. Her parents treat her like a scab that should be picked off and flicked away. Worse than her parents is the evil headmistress, or principal, who rules Matilda's school. She is out to get little kids. But don't feel too bad for Matilda. She may be misunderstood, but she outsmarts everyone. The story is about how you can always turn your life around, no matter how tough it is.

Matilda's parents are awful. Her father breaks the law by selling used cars that break down as soon as they are sold. Her mother rushes off to her bingo games, leaving Matilda alone all day. Each night, the whole family has to sit in front of the "boob tube." The "boob tube" is the TV. And dinner is just warmed-up frozen meals.

The school's headmistress, Miss Trunchbull, is even worse than Matilda's parents. She was once an Olympic athlete. Now she is just **deranged**, or crazy! In school, Miss Trunchbull uses her strength to throw helpless children out the window. She punishes them by locking them in a tiny cupboard called "The Chokey." It has sharp glass on the walls. She terrifies everyone.

There are only two nice adults in this book. They are the librarian who becomes friends with Matilda and her first teacher, Miss Jennifer Honey.

Miss Honey is kind to everybody, but she doesn't have any backbone. That means she doesn't stand up for herself. She's afraid of Miss Trunchbull, though I can't say I blame her!

Miss Honey lives in a tiny house that is like a prison. There is no heat. There is no kitchen and there is hardly any food. The house has wooden boxes for furniture. Why can't Miss Honey afford to live in a nice house? That's one of the mysteries for readers to solve.

I liked the children in this book, especially Matilda. She is supersmart. She teaches herself how to read. She does complicated math problems in her head.

Matilda is a terrific book. It teaches readers a valuable lesson. So what if you come from a terrible home? You can use the power inside yourself to make things better. That's what Matilda does. She comes up with a secret plan to save the day. When she goes into action, everybody is shocked and stunned, especially Miss Trunchbull. Seeing the headmistress more frightened than the children she tries to scare is great! Read the book for yourself and see. I think everyone should read *Matilda*, even—or maybe especially!— adults.

Matilda: Book Review

Poor Matilda! Her father and mother treat her like a scab that should be picked off and flicked away. Worse, an evil headmistress who is out to get little kids rules Matilda's school. But don't feel too bad for Matilda. She may be misunderstood, but she outsmarts everyone.

Matilda, a children's book by British author Roald Dahl, was published in 1988. It's a story about an unhappy genius trapped in a rotten family. It shows how you can turn your life around, no matter how tough it is.

Matilda's parents are utterly awful. Matilda's father violates the law by selling used cars that break down as soon as they are driven off the lot. Her mother rushes off to her bingo games, leaving Matilda alone all day. Each night, the whole family has to sit in front of the "boob tube." And dinner consists of warmed-up frozen meals.

If anyone could be worse than Matilda's parents, it is the school's headmistress, Miss Trunchbull. She was once an Olympic athlete. Now she is just deranged! Dahl paints her vividly with words. In school, she uses her strength to throw helpless children out the window. She punishes them by locking them in a tiny cupboard with sharp glass on the walls called "The Chokey." She terrifies everyone.

The only nice adults in this novel are the librarian who befriends Matilda and her first teacher, Miss Jennifer Honey. Miss Honey is kind to everybody, but she doesn't have any backbone. She's afraid of Miss Trunchbull and can't stand up to her, though I can't say I blame her!

Miss Honey lives in a tiny house that is like a prison. There is no heat or kitchen. There is hardly any food. The house has wooden boxes for furniture. Why can't Miss Honey afford to live in a nice house? That's one of the key mysteries in the book for readers to solve.

I liked the children in this book, especially Matilda. She is off-the-charts smart. She teaches herself how to read. She does complicated math problems in her head.

Matilda is a terrific book. It teaches readers a valuable lesson. So what if you come from a terrible home? You can summon the power inside yourself to make things better. That's what Matilda does. She comes up with a secret plan to save the day. When she goes into action, everybody is shocked and stunned, especially Miss Trunchbull. There's nothing better than seeing the headmistress more frightened than the children she tries to scare! Read the book for yourself and see. As far as I'm concerned, everyone should read *Matilda*, even— or maybe especially!—adults.

Matilda: Book Review

Poor Matilda! Her father and mother treat her like a scab that should be picked off and flicked away. Worse, an evil headmistress who is out to get little kids rules Matilda's school. But don't feel too bad for Matilda. She may be misunderstood, but she outsmarts everyone.

Matilda, a children's book by British author Roald Dahl, was published in 1988. It's a story about an unhappy genius trapped in a rotten family. It shows how you can turn your life around, no matter how tough it is.

Matilda's parents are utterly awful. Matilda's father violates the law by selling used cars that break down as soon as they are driven off the lot. Her mother rushes off to her bingo games, leaving Matilda alone all day. Each night, the whole family has to sit in front of the "boob tube." And dinner consists of warmed-up frozen meals.

If anyone could be worse than Matilda's parents, it is the school's headmistress, Miss Trunchbull. She was once an Olympic athlete. Now she is just deranged! Dahl paints her vividly with words. In school, she uses her strength to throw helpless children out the window. She punishes them by locking them in a tiny cupboard with sharp glass on the walls called "The Chokey." She terrifies everyone.

The only nice adults in this novel are the librarian who befriends Matilda and her first teacher, Miss Jennifer Honey. Miss Honey is kind to everybody, but she doesn't have any backbone. She's afraid of Miss Trunchbull and can't stand up to her, though I can't say I blame her!

Miss Honey lives in a tiny house that is like a prison. There is no heat or kitchen. There is hardly any food. The house has wooden boxes for furniture. Why can't Miss Honey afford to live in a nice house? That's one of the key mysteries in the book for readers to solve.

I liked the children in this book, especially Matilda. She is off-the-charts smart. She teaches herself how to read. She does complicated math problems in her head.

Matilda is a terrific book. It teaches readers a valuable lesson. So what if you come from a terrible home? You can summon the power inside yourself to make things better. That's what Matilda does. She comes up with a secret plan to save the day. When she goes into action, everybody is shocked and stunned, especially Miss Trunchbull. There's nothing better than seeing the headmistress more frightened than the children she tries to scare! Read the book for yourself and see. As far as I'm concerned, everyone should read *Matilda*, even—or maybe especially!— adults.

Name _____ Date _____

Use what you read in the passage to answer the questions.

1. Who wrote *Matilda*?

_____

_____

2. Why is Matilda unhappy?

_____

_____

3. In what ways are Matilda's parents awful?

_____

_____

4. What does **deranged** mean?

_____

_____

5. What details show you how mean Miss Trunchbull is?

_____

_____

6. What does Matilda think of Miss Honey?

_____

_____

7. What is the writer's purpose in writing this review?

_____

_____

8. Why would or wouldn't you read this book?

_____

_____

Matilda: Film Review

If you like the book *Matilda* by Roald Dahl, you will love the 1996 movie. Like the book, the movie is about a girl who is a genius but is misunderstood. Her family is awful and she goes to a terrible school.

The **screenwriters**, or people who wrote the movie, are Nicholas Kazan and Robin Swicord. They were pretty true to Dahl's book. Danny DeVito is both the movie director and one of the lead actors. DeVito put together a great cast that includes his wife, actress Rhea Perlman. They are hilarious together as Matilda's parents. They dress like clowns, eat like pigs, and care only about themselves. The looks on their faces will make you laugh every time!

Pam Ferris plays the part of cruel Miss Trunchbull, the abusive and ugly headmistress of Crunchem Hall Elementary School. As Miss Trunchbull, Ferris carries a horseback-riding crop, or whip, to scare the children.

The actress Mara Wilson plays the role of Matilda as a nice kid but no pushover. When Matilda's father is mean, she fights back. One night, Matilda's dad is angry with her for reading books and not watching TV. He grabs her head and forces her to watch. But Matilda has her revenge. She uses her special mental powers to make the TV explode. Matilda is a take-charge kid! She realizes her parents aren't really going to do much for her. She doesn't cry about it. Instead, she takes care of herself and has fun.

The screenwriters weren't afraid to take chances. They added two major **subplots**, or smaller stories within the bigger story. Including subplots meant adding more scenes to enhance the character or action.

The first subplot is about a pair of goofy undercover FBI agents who watch Matilda's home. Her clueless parents don't realize they're being watched day and night. The agents hope to catch Matilda's father selling "lemons" and then arrest him. Matilda warns her parents, but do they listen?

The second subplot involves Matilda getting back at Miss Trunchbull for treating her badly. She creeps into Miss Trunchbull's home. She makes it so the headmistress thinks her house is haunted. The next day, Matilda uses her special powers to write a ghostly message on the board. She also makes two erasers attack Miss Trunchbull. Then the other kids get in on the action. They give the headmistress a send-off she will never forget.

You'll want to watch this movie over and over. Matilda becomes a real-life superhero!

Matilda: Film Review

How often do you see a movie and think the book is so much better? Well, you won't have to worry about that with the movie version of *Matilda*. This movie really delivers!

Roald Dahl's book is a modern children's classic. Matilda is a misunderstood genius who lives in an awful family and goes to a terrible school. Screenwriters Nicholas Kazan and Robin Swicord are pretty faithful to Dahl's story in their 1996 movie. But they also add a little magic of their own!

Hats off to Danny DeVito, the director and one of the lead actors. He's brought a great cast together. He and his actress wife, Rhea Perlman, play the parents of Matilda, and they are hilarious. They dress like clowns, eat like pigs, and care only about themselves. The looks on their faces will make you laugh every time!

Pam Ferris plays the cruel and abusive headmistress of Crunchem Hall Elementary School, Miss Trunchbull. As Miss Trunchbull, Ferris turns herself into a frightening headmistress who's both massive and ugly and carries a horseback-riding crop to scare everybody.

Mara Wilson plays Matilda as a nice kid, but she's no pushover. When her father is mean to her, she strikes back. One night, Matilda's dad is so angry with his daughter for reading books and not watching TV that he grabs her head and forces her to watch. But Matilda gets her revenge by using her special mental powers to make the TV explode. Matilda is a take-charge kid! She realizes her parents aren't really going to do much for her. She doesn't cry about it. She just goes her own way and has fun.

The screenwriters weren't afraid to take chances, either. They added two major subplots to the movie. The first subplot is about a pair of goofy undercover FBI agents watching Matilda's home. Her parents are clueless that they're being watched day and night. The agents want proof to bust Matilda's father for his shady used-car business. Matilda warns her parents, but do they listen?

The second subplot involves Matilda getting revenge on Miss Trunchbull. She creeps into Miss Trunchbull's home and fixes it so the headmistress thinks the house is haunted. The next day, Matilda uses her powers not only to write a ghostly message on the board, but she also makes two erasers attack Miss Trunchbull. Then the other kids get in on the action. They give the headmistress a send-off she will never forget.

This is a film you'll want to watch over and over. You'll have a good laugh at these funny actors and enjoy how Matilda becomes a real-life superhero!

Matilda: Film Review

How often do you see a movie and think the book is so much better? Well, you won't have to worry about that with the movie version of *Matilda*. This movie really delivers!

Roald Dahl's book is a modern children's classic. Matilda is a misunderstood genius who lives with a terrible family and goes to a horrible school. Screenwriters Nicholas Kazan and Robin Swicord are pretty faithful to Dahl's story in their 1996 movie, but they also add a little magic of their own!

Hats off to Danny DeVito, the director and one of the lead actors. He's brought a great cast together, including his actress wife, Rhea Perlman. DeVito and Perlman play the parents of Matilda, and they are hilarious. They dress like clowns, eat like pigs, and care only about themselves. The looks on their faces will make you laugh every time!

Pam Ferris plays the cruel and abusive headmistress of Crunchem Hall Elementary School, Miss Trunchbull. As Miss Trunchbull, Ferris turns herself into a frightening headmistress who's both massive and ugly, and carries a horseback-riding crop to scare everybody.

Mara Wilson plays Matilda, who is a nice kid, but in no way is she a pushover. Whenever her father is mean to her, Matilda strikes back. One night, Matilda's dad is so angry with her for reading books and not watching television that he grabs her head and forces her to watch the show. But Matilda gets her revenge by using her special mental powers to make the television explode, proving herself to be a take-charge kid! She realizes her parents aren't really going to do much for her, so she doesn't cry about it. She just goes her own way and has fun.

The screenwriters weren't afraid to take chances, either. They added two major subplots to the movie. The first subplot is about a pair of goofy undercover FBI agents watching Matilda's home. Her parents are clueless that they're being watched day and night. The agents want proof to bust Matilda's father for his shady used-car business. Matilda warns her parents, but they don't listen.

The second subplot involves Matilda getting revenge on Miss Trunchbull. She creeps into Miss Trunchbull's home and fixes it so the headmistress thinks her house is haunted. The next day, Matilda uses her powers not only to write a ghostly message on the board, but she also makes two erasers attack Miss Trunchbull. Then the other kids get in on the action and give the headmistress a send-off she will never forget.

This is a film you'll want to watch over and over. You'll have a good laugh at these funny actors and enjoy how Matilda becomes a real-life superhero!

Name _____ Date _____

Use what you read in the passage to answer the questions.

1. What are **screenwriters**?

_____

_____

2. What clues help you infer that the reviewer liked DeVito and Perlman as Matilda's parents?

_____

_____

3. What does Miss Trunchbull carry to scare everybody?

_____

_____

4. What is Matilda's father's job?

_____

_____

5. What kind of kid is Matilda? What clues help you draw this conclusion?

_____

_____

6. What does the word **subplots** mean in this movie?

_____

_____

7. What clues in this review support the conclusion that this movie may be too frightening for young children?

_____

_____

8. Does the writer want you to see the film *Matilda*? How do you know?

_____

_____

What is an advertisement?

An advertisement, or "ad," is a form of persuasive communication. It may include writing, images, or both. For written ads, the writer tries to persuade his or her audience to buy or do something. The writer tells what is good about a product or service. The writer also tries to persuade people that they need this product or service. The writer uses description and details.

What is the purpose of an advertisement?

People write advertisements to sell products. The goal of an ad is to persuade others to buy or use certain goods or services. Ads tell people about different products. Some ads explain how a product works or tell why one product is better than another. Other ads explain how a product or service can help solve a problem or make people's lives better. Often, ads try to entertain people or make a lasting impression in some way so that people will remember to buy the product.

Who is the audience for an advertisement?

The audience for an advertisement is the consumer, or person who buys things. A specific consumer audience is identified and targeted depending on the product or service being sold. It also depends on where the ad is printed. The audience will be people interested in that product. The ad writer wants to *reach*, or speak to, all the people who might want to buy the product, but the writer may change the ad depending on the type of person likely to read the ad. For example, if the ad is in a kids' magazine, it will try to appeal to a younger audience than if the ad is in a parents' magazine.

How do you read an advertisement?

Pay attention to the product or service being sold and how the writer is trying to sell it. Does the ad writer do a good job? Does the ad leave a lasting impression? Does the writer convince you that you want or perhaps even *need* the product? Do you believe that the product is good and is something that will improve your life? If yes, why? What did the writer say that convinced you? Did he or she give good facts, detail, and reasons for why this was a good product? What made you want to buy it?

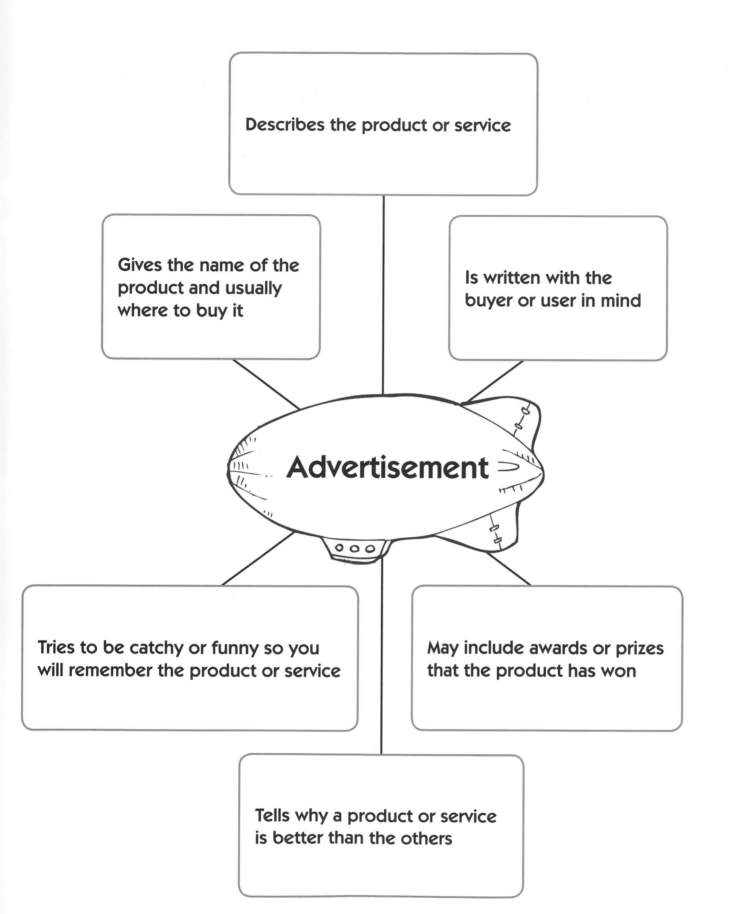

Describes the product or service

Gives the name of the product and usually where to buy it

Is written with the buyer or user in mind

Advertisement

Tries to be catchy or funny so you will remember the product or service

May include awards or prizes that the product has won

Tells why a product or service is better than the others

Become a Chess Master

Chess is a very hard game to play. The opponents, or people who play against each other, come up with ways to challenge each other. Although it is a hard game, people have been playing it for two hundred years!

If you like chess, you will love Chess Mess. This updated version of chess is the newest board game to hit the market. Chess Mess is just like the old game but with a new twist.

The game board comes with four water spouts. There is one spout in each corner. Water shoots into your opponent's face when you take a chess piece from him or her. The spray is like saying, "Ha-ha. Got you!" When you check your opponent, water comes out of TWO spouts, sending double splashes at your opponent's face. A check is when you put one of your pieces in position to capture your opponent's king. Can you guess what happens when you win? You got it! All four spouts spray your opponent in defeat. Chess Mess is ready for every trick up your sleeve. The board knows over a thousand moves. It is always ready to spray you for one wrong play.

Chess Mess is easy to put together. Each side of the game board has a nozzle to put in water.

Bobby Fischer wannabes will never know what hit them with Chess Mess! There's no better way to become the next grand master than using Chess Mess.

Become a Chess Master

Chess is one of the most difficult games in our world's history. It involves opponents challenging each other with different plays. It's a hard game to master, but it has kept people entertained for two hundred years.

If you like the game of chess, you are going to love Chess Mess. This modern version of chess is the newest board game to hit the market. Chess Mess offers the same mental challenges as the traditional game while providing hours of fun.

The game board comes with four spouts—one in each corner. Water shoots out from a spout into your opponent's face when you take a piece. As if your opponent doesn't feel bad enough, the spray is like saying, "Ha-ha. Got you!" When you check your opponent, water comes out of not one, but TWO spouts, sending double splashes at your opponent's face. Can you guess what happens when you win? You got it! All four spouts shower your opponent in defeat. Chess Mess is ready for every trick up your sleeve. The board knows over a thousand moves and is at the ready to unleash its punishment for one wrong play.

Chess Mess is easy to assemble, or put together. Each side of the game board has a nozzle for easy access to the spouts.

Bobby Fischer wannabes will never know what hit them with Chess Mess! There's no better way to become the next grand master than using Chess Mess.

Become a Chess Master

Chess is one the most mentally challenging games in our world's history. The two-hundred-year-old game requires players to put their brains in high gear to overcome each hurdle set against them by their opponents. If you liked chess before, you are going to love it now. That's because Chess Mess, the newest board game to hit the market, is bringing the game of chess into the twenty-first century. Chess Mess offers the same mental challenges as the traditional game while providing hours of entertainment.

The game board comes equipped with four spouts—one in each corner. Just when your opponent is feeling down about your taking his piece, water shoots out from one spout into his face, as if to say "Ha-ha. Got you!" As a double whammy, when you check your opponent, two spouts activate, sending double splashes at his face. And what do you imagine happens when you checkmate your opponents? You got it! All four spouts go at once, showering your opponent in defeat. To make the game even more exciting, Chess Mess is ready for every trick up your sleeve. The board recognizes over a thousand moves and is at the ready to unleash its punishment for one wrong play.

Chess Mess is easy to assemble and use. Each side of the board has a nozzle for easy access to fill up each spout.

Bobby Fischer wannabes will never know what hit them with Chess Mess! There's no better way to train to become the next grand master than using Chess Mess.

◼ ●●●

Name _____ Date _____

Use what you read in the passage to answer the questions.

1. What is this ad for?

_____

_____

2. How old is the game of chess?

_____

_____

3. What makes Chess Mess different than regular chess?

_____

_____

4. When does Chess Mess spray from two spouts?

_____

_____

5. What happens when you make a wrong move?

_____

_____

6. How many spouts are there?

_____

_____

7. How do you get water into the game board?

_____

_____

8. Who was Bobby Fischer?

_____

_____

Butterflies in Your Stomach

Have you ever had "butterflies in your stomach"? You know, that tickly feeling when you're nervous or scared. You might feel it before a big test or championship game. Now you really can have butterflies in your stomach with a brand-new, super-awesome candy called Whim Whams. Whim Whams are small butterfly-shaped jelly candies. After you eat them, they flutter in your stomach. First you swallow a Whim Wham, then you wait a moment, and soon you'll feel a tickle in your tummy. The tickle keeps going as long as you keep eating Whim Whams.

Whim Whams come in lots of different flavors: Bouncing Berry, Frazzled Fruit, Sour Skittishness, and Hot Heebie-Jeebies. Have fun with your food even after you eat with Whim Whams!

Whim Whams are great for birthday parties or any party. Try this game with your guests: Mix Whim Whams into a bowl of candy. Invite everyone to eat a piece. Then try to guess who has eaten the fluttering candies!

Whim Whams are a new way to enjoy candy! Whim Whams—the candy that is causing a flutter of excitement!

Butterflies in Your Stomach

You've heard the saying "butterflies in your stomach." It's used to describe that fluttery feeling you get in your stomach before a big test, a championship game, or other important events. Well, now you really can have butterflies in your stomach with a brand-new, super-awesome candy called Whim Whams. Whim Whams are small butterfly-shaped jelly candies that flutter in your stomach after you eat them. Swallow some Whim Whams and wait a few moments. Soon you'll feel a tickle in your tummy. The tickle continues as long as you keep eating Whim Whams.

Whim Whams come in a variety of flavors: Bouncing Berry, Frazzled Fruit, Sour Skittishness, and for those with a spicy tooth, Hot Heebie-Jeebies. Whim Whams let you have fun with your food even after you eat!

Whim Whams are great for birthday parties or any party. Try this game with your guests: Mix Whim Whams into a bowl of candy. Invite everyone to eat a piece. Then try to guess who has eaten the fluttering candies!

A new way to enjoy candy is here and ready for action! Enjoy Whim Whams—the candy that is causing a flutter of excitement!

Butterflies in Your Stomach

You know that funny feeling you get in your stomach before something important, like a championship playoff or a big test? You've probably heard this funny feeling described as having "butterflies in your stomach." Well, now you really can have butterflies in your stomach! Try our new and super-awesome Whim Whams. Whim Whams are small butterfly-shaped jelly candies that flutter in your stomach after you eat them. After swallowing some Whim Whams, wait a few moments. You'll soon feel a flutter or tickle in your tummy. The tickle continues as long as you keep eating Whim Whams.

Whim Whams come in a variety of flavors, including Bouncing Berry, Frazzled Fruit, Sour Skittishness, and for those with a spicy tooth, Hot Heebie-Jeebies. With Whim Whams, you have fun with your food even after you've eaten!

Whim Whams are the perfect treat for birthday parties or any party. Try this game at your next party: Mix Whim Whams into a bowl of candy and see who has eaten the fluttering candies!

A new way to enjoy candy is here and ready for action! Enjoy new Whim Whams—the candy that is causing a flutter of excitement!

●●●

Name _____ Date _____

Use what you read in the passage to answer the questions.

1. What does it mean to have "butterflies in your stomach"?

_____

_____

2. What causes you to have butterflies in your stomach?

_____

_____

3. What kind of food are Whim Whams?

_____

_____

4. What do Whim Whams look like?

_____

_____

5. What happens if you keep eating Whim Whams?

_____

_____

6. What are two Whim Whams flavors?

_____

_____

7. What happens after you swallow a Whim Wham?

_____

_____

8. Would you buy Whim Whams? Why or why not?

_____

_____

Unit 10 Mini-Lesson
Speeches

What is a speech?

A speech is a written document that is recited, or read aloud. A speech tries to convince readers to believe or do something. A speech, like other persuasive texts, often has a strong point of view about an idea or a problem. It includes facts and examples to support an opinion, and it usually suggests a solution.

What is the purpose of a speech?

People write speeches to "sway," or change the minds of, their audience. They want their audience to see their points of view. They may want to motivate, or encourage people to take action, too. The purpose of a political speech might be to change public opinion or persuade people to vote for something or someone. Other speeches are written to inspire, celebrate, or simply thank people.

Who is the audience for a speech?

People write speeches for all types of occasions, including political rallies, award ceremonies, weddings, funerals, and even birthday parties. People write speeches to share their views, and tell people about something they believe in. They may write a speech to gain support for a person or a cause. They may also write a speech to convince their audience to act in favor of or against something.

How do you read (or listen to) a speech?

Keep in mind that the speaker or speech writer wants you to support his or her position. Ask yourself: *What is this person's position, or opinion? Does she support it with facts and good reasons? Do I agree with her?* A good speech writer knows her audience. She uses facts and reasons that might sway her audience in her favor. She also reads the speech aloud several times to make sure that the words are powerful and flow when spoken.

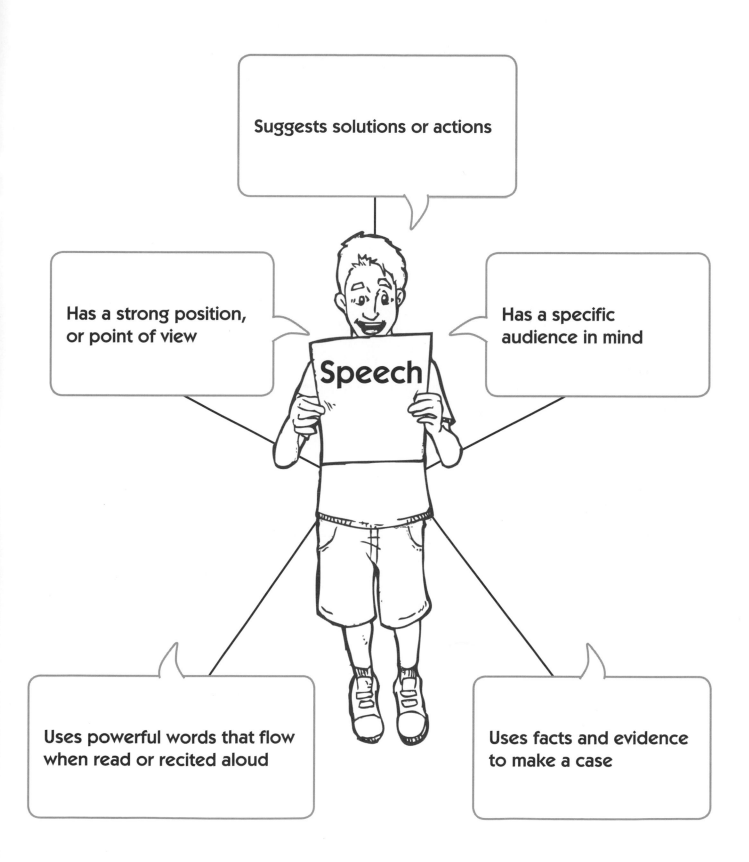

My Fellow Engineers!

We use fossil fuels every day. Coal is a fossil fuel. It is used to make electricity for our alarm clocks, microwaves, computers, and more. Oil is another fossil fuel. It is used to power cars, trucks, buses, planes, and trains. Natural gas is also a fossil fuel. We use it to warm our homes and cook our food. Fossil fuels can do all of these jobs. They are easy to control, transport, change, and burn. Other energy sources, such as solar, wind, water, and nuclear power, make only electricity. They are not able to power most types of transportation. There is no other energy source as useful as fossil fuels. Fossil fuels are America's best source of power.

Our need for energy is constant. Fossil fuels are amazingly **diverse**. They are able to do more tasks than any other source of energy. And fossil fuels are by far the most affordable source of energy on the planet.

Some groups have criticized the use of fossil fuels. They say fossil fuels cause problems such as air pollution and climate change. They believe that renewable resources are better for the environment. But every source of energy has some environmental problem. Solar cells are made with poisonous metals. Wind turbines kill birds. They also cause noise pollution.

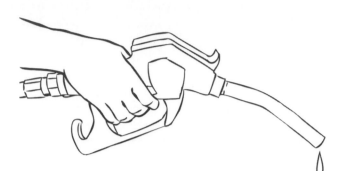

Even hydropower dams cause problems. They drown rivers and animals that depend on the water—from endangered amphibians to fish that can no longer swim upstream to spawn, or deposit eggs.

Fossil fuels are made to be clean and safe. Clean-coal technology takes the dirt out of raw coal long before it is able to reach the power plant. Scrubbing smokestacks removes the remaining pollutants.

For more than 100 years, fossil fuels have been the world's most used energy source. Billions of people depend on them every day. They make energy steadily, predictably, and on demand. And the cost simply can't be beat. They make power affordable for everyone. Fossil fuels make our way of life possible. And technology makes sure fossil fuels will be environmentally sustainable for years to come. It makes sense that we continue to use fossil fuels. They are the best source of power on the planet.

My Fellow Engineers!

We use fossil fuels every day. Coal is a fossil fuel. We use it to make electricity for our alarm clocks, microwaves, computers, and more. Oil is another fossil fuel. Oil powers cars, trucks, buses, planes, and trains. Natural gas is also a fossil fuel. We use it to warm our homes and cook our food. Fossil fuels can do all of these jobs because they are easy to control, transport, change, and burn. Other energy sources, such as solar, wind, water, and nuclear power, make only electricity. They are not able to power most types of transportation. There is no other energy source as useful as fossil fuels. Fossil fuels are America's best source of power.

Our need for energy is constant, and fossil fuels are amazingly diverse. They are able to do more tasks than any other source of energy. In addition, fossil fuels are by far the most affordable source of energy on the planet.

Some groups have criticized fossil fuels. They say fossil fuels cause problems such as air pollution and climate change. They believe that renewable resources are better for the environment. The truth is, every source of energy has some environmental problem. Solar cells are made with poisonous metals. Wind turbines kill birds. They also cause noise pollution. Even hydropower dams cause problems. They drown rivers and animals that depend on the water, from endangered amphibians to fish that can no longer swim upstream to spawn, or deposit eggs.

Fossil fuels, however, are made to be clean and safe. Clean-coal technology takes impurities out of raw coal long before they are able to reach the power plant. Scrubbing smokestacks removes the remaining pollutants.

For more than 100 years, fossil fuels have been the world's most used energy source. Billions of people depend on them every day. They make energy steadily, predictably, and on demand. And their cost simply can't be beat. They make power affordable for everyone. Fossil fuels make our way of life possible. And technology makes sure fossil fuels will be environmentally sustainable for decades to come. It makes sense that we continue to use fossil fuels. They are the best source of power on the planet.

My Fellow Engineers!

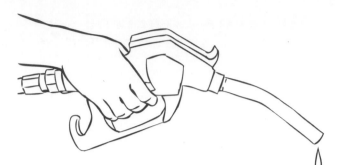

We use fossil fuels every day. Coal is a fossil fuel that is used to make electricity for our alarm clocks, microwaves, computers, and more. Oil is another fossil fuel, and it is used to power cars, trucks, buses, planes, and trains. Natural gas is also a fossil fuel. We use it to warm our homes and cook our food. Fossil fuels can do all of these jobs because they are easy to control, transport, change, and burn. Other energy sources, such as solar, wind, water, and nuclear power, make only electricity and therefore are not able to power most types of transportation. There is no other energy source as useful as fossil fuels. Fossil fuels are America's best source of power.

Our need for energy is constant, and fossil fuels are amazingly diverse. They are able to do more tasks than any other source of energy. In addition, fossil fuels are by far the most affordable source of energy on the planet.

Some groups have criticized the use of fossil fuels. They say fossil fuels cause problems such as air pollution and climate change. They believe that renewable resources are better for the environment. The truth is that every source of energy has some environmental problem; solar cells are made with poisonous metals and wind turbines kill birds and cause noise pollution. Even hydropower dams cause problems—they drown rivers and animals that depend on the water, from endangered amphibians to fish that can no longer swim upstream to spawn, or deposit eggs.

Fossil fuels, however, are made to be clean and safe. Clean-coal technology takes impurities out of raw coal long before they are able to reach the power plant. Scrubbing smokestacks removes the remaining pollutants.

For more than 100 years, fossil fuels have been the world's most used energy source. Billions of people depend on them every day. They make energy steadily, predictably, and on demand, and their cost simply can't be beat. They make power affordable for everyone. Fossil fuels make our way of life possible. And technology makes sure fossil fuels will be environmentally sustainable for decades to come. It makes sense that we continue to use fossil fuels. They are the best source of power on the planet.

Name _____ Date _____

Use what you read in the passage to answer the questions.

1. Who is the audience of this speech?

_____

_____

2. What are two examples of fossil fuels?

_____

_____

3. What do we use natural gas for?

_____

_____

4. In what way is solar power limiting?

_____

_____

5. What does the word **diverse** mean?

_____

_____

6. What problems do critics say fossil fuels cause?

_____

_____

7. What is an example of a renewable source of energy?

_____

_____

8. What makes the speaker persuasive or convincing? Give examples.

_____

_____

My Fellow Senators!

Imagine finding the perfect source of energy. Now picture that this power source never runs out. It is available everywhere on the planet. People could make electricity in their own backyards! There's no need to imagine. This energy source is real. It's called renewable energy and there are not just one but three major kinds. They are solar, wind, and water power. Renewable energy is our best source for making electricity because it IS renewable. That means it will never run out. It is also available everywhere, and it's safe for the environment.

Most other energy resources are nonrenewable. Fossil fuels are nonrenewable. Once we burn fossil fuels, such as coal, oil, or natural gas, they are gone forever. But sun, wind, and water aren't destroyed as we use them.

Solar cells change sunlight into electricity. They are flat panels that can go anywhere the sun shines. They turn schools, homes, offices, and even parking lots into private power plants. One-fifth of America's electricity comes from hydropower. Hydropower is energy from water. The U.S. Department of Energy has found over 5,000 places where we could build new hydropower stations on local rivers.

Fossil fuels and uranium, the fuel for nuclear power, are found only in certain parts of the world. Most of those places are outside the United States. Today we spend billions of dollars on fossil fuels, especially oil. The money goes to support dangerous dictators and nations that wish America harm. Using local renewable resources instead is a smart move for our national safety.

Renewable energy is the most environmentally friendly source of power. This is true especially compared to fossil fuels and nuclear energy. Drilling and shipping oil often lead to spills. Spills hurt wildlife. They also harm the fishing industry. Fishing depends on healthy seas, tourism, and other local economies. Nuclear energy creates deadly, cancer-causing, radioactive waste. We also haven't found a place to safely store nuclear waste.

What if the wind stops blowing or the sun goes down? Luckily the sun and wind never stop producing power everywhere all at once. And America has electrical wires that move energy from where it's made to where it's needed at any moment. While the sun is down in the evening in New York, it still shines brightly on solar cells in California.

Critics of renewable energy also ignore hydropower. Hydropower runs 24 hours a day, 7 days a week, 365 days a year.

Fossil fuels and nuclear fuel will run out one day. But the more renewable energy we use, the more energy we get in return!

My Fellow Senators!

Can you imagine finding the perfect source of energy? This amazing power source would be one that never runs out. It would be available everywhere on the planet so people could make electricity in their own backyards. Well, you don't need to imagine this because it's real. It's called renewable energy. And there is not one but three major kinds of renewable energy: solar, wind, and water power. Renewable energy is our best source of energy for making electricity because it IS renewable. That means it will never run out because we renew it. It is also widely available and safe for the environment.

Most other energy resources, such as fossil fuels, are nonrenewable. Once we burn fossil fuels such as coal, oil, or natural gas, they are gone. But sun, wind, and water aren't destroyed as we use them.

Solar cells are flat panels that change sunlight into electricity. They can go anywhere the sun shines. They turn schools, homes, offices, even parking lots into private power plants. One-fifth of America's electricity comes from water, or hydropower. And the U.S. Department of Energy has found over 5,000 places across the nation where we could build new hydropower stations on local rivers.

Fossil fuels and uranium, the fuel for nuclear power, are found only in certain parts of the world. Most of those places are outside the United States. Today we spend billions of dollars on fossil fuels, especially oil. The money we spend on these energy sources supports dangerous dictators and nations that wish America harm. Switching to local renewable resources is a smart move for our national safety.

Renewable energy is clearly the most environmentally friendly source of power. This is true especially compared with fossil fuels and nuclear energy. Drilling and shipping oil frequently lead to spills. These spills threaten wildlife. They also harm the fishing industry, which depends on healthy seas, tourism, and other local economies. Nuclear energy creates deadly, cancer-causing, radioactive waste. We also haven't found a place to safely store nuclear waste. So it simply piles up at the nuclear power plants.

What if the wind stops blowing or the sun goes down? In reality, the sun and wind never stop producing power everywhere all at once. And America's grid of electrical wires moves energy from where it's made to where it's needed at any moment. While the sun is down in the evening in New York, it still shines brightly on solar cells in California.

Critics of renewable energy also ignore hydropower, which runs 24 hours a day, 7 days a week, 365 days a year.

Fossil fuels and nuclear fuel will run out one day. However, the more renewable energy we use, the more plentiful that energy becomes!

My Fellow Senators!

Imagine discovering the perfect source of electricity, a miraculous power source that will never run out. It can be found absolutely anywhere on the planet so people can make electricity in their own backyards. It's called renewable energy, and there are not one but three major kinds. Solar, wind, and water power are our best sources of energy for making electricity. Each is totally limitless, widely available, and environmentally safe.

Most other energy resources, including fossil fuels, are nonrenewable. Once we take energy from nuclear fuel or burn coal, oil, or natural gas, those fuels are used up forever. But sun, wind, and water aren't destroyed as we use them.

Solar cells, flat panels that convert sunlight into electricity, can go anywhere the sun shines. They can turn schools, homes, and even parking lots into private power plants. Hydropower already provides one-fifth of America's electricity. The U.S. Department of Energy has found over 5,000 places where we could build new hydropower stations on local rivers. Wind power is just as convenient.

Fossil fuels and uranium, the fuel for nuclear power, are found only in certain parts of the world. But many of those places are outside the United States. Today we spend billions of dollars on fossil fuels, especially oil.

This supports dangerous dictators and nations. Switching to local renewable resources is a smart move for our national safety.

No matter how you look at it, renewable energy is the most environmentally friendly source of power, especially compared with fossil fuels and nuclear energy. Drilling and shipping oil frequently lead to spills that threaten not only wildlife, but the fishing industry as well. That industry depends on healthy seas, tourism, and other local economies. Nuclear energy creates deadly cancer-causing radioactive waste, and we have yet to find a place to store it safely. So it simply piles up at the nuclear power plants.

What happens if the wind stops blowing or the sun goes down? Our vast grid of electrical wires moves energy from where it's made to where it's needed at any moment. While the sun is down in the evening in New York, it still shines brightly on solar cells in California.

These same critics ignore hydropower as well, which runs 24 hours a day, 7 days a week, 365 days a year. In fact, the truly impractical energy source is fossil fuels. Fossil fuels and nuclear fuel are nonrenewable. On the other hand, the more renewable energy we use, the more plentiful it becomes!

Name _____ Date _____

Use what you read in the passage to answer the questions.

1. How many major kinds of renewable energy sources are there?

_____

_____

2. Why does the speaker say renewable energy is the best source for making electricity?

_____

_____

3. What happens to nonrenewable resources after we use them?

_____

_____

4. What do solar cells do?

_____

_____

5. How much of America's electricity is already provided by hydropower?

_____

_____

6. In what way do you think we are supporting dangerous dictators when we use fossil fuels?

_____

_____

7. Which energy source causes cancer and radioactive waste?

_____

_____

8. What was the most persuasive or convincing part of this speech? How so?

_____

_____

Answer Key

Unit 1 Memoirs I
page 13

1. Separating people based on race
2. 1944
3. He left Poland in 1910 because he did not want to fight in the army.
4. Grandpa David was a very accepting and open-minded person. He was very kind and treated people right. For example, he took in a homeless man and fed him once a week at his home.
5. Stokely Carmichael is a close school friend of the author. He was a future activist who participated in demonstrations against segregation in New York City with the Freedom Riders. He influenced the author to start participating in demonstrations and activism while they were in high school together.
6. Answers will vary.
7. Macy's would not hire African Americans to work in its store.
8. The writer would regularly participate in demonstrations or picket for causes that she believed in to promote peace and equality.

Unit 1 Memoirs II
page 17

1. Money that pays for an education
2. Mary lived across the hall from the writer's apartment.
3. The writer started high school at Spellman.
4. At Spellman he'd get a better education and be more prepared for college.
5. The writer wanted to go to the nearby high school with the neighborhood kids. The writer "gave in" after feeling the decision was made for him by his teacher.
6. She smiled at the writer.
7. His heart was pounding.
8. He met a lot of kids just like him. Nobody cared about what he wasn't good at. They just liked him for who he was.

Unit 2 Historical Fiction I
page 23

1. Belshunu had offered Ditanu an apprenticeship, as well as a home.
2. A stone carver
3. He was studying a craft and did not live with his violent uncle anymore.
4. Ditanu felt perfectly happy and thought his future looked bright now that he did not live with Lamusa.
5. Wife of Hudu-libbi
6. A commissioned statue similar to those found in the hearts of temples
7. So they could pray constantly to the gods
8. Ditanu meant his future looked like it was set and no longer changeable.

Answer Key

Unit 2 Historical Fiction II
page 27

1. September 11, 2001
2. He turned on the TV and it was the first thing he saw. It seems just like a movie and not real life.
3. The thirty-first floor of the North Tower in the World Trade Center
4. She was two blocks away when the North Tower was hit.
5. The building collapsed.
6. He was relieved that his mother was okay.
7. The Pentagon
8. Answers will vary.

Unit 3 Myths
page 33

1. To notice nothingness, and picture how it was before Ra created the world
2. The black sea
3. A great city
4. Answers will vary.
5. They would bring joy to him in youth and care for him in his old age.
6. He sneezed
7. The goddess of moisture and rain
8. Happy

Unit 3 Legends
page 37

1. The Greek god who ruled the sea, storms, and earthquakes
2. Kind
3. Poseidon and Cleito's eldest son, Atlas
4. They felt that they didn't have any sorrow or suffering in their nation because they were better, smarter, more honest, and harder workers than other nations.
5. The Atlanteans fought and conquered every nation they came across.
6. Atlas created the most powerful explosion ever felt by the nation.
7. Atlantis disappeared into the sea, sunk by its own selfishness.
8. To never gloat or be to proud, nor take for granted what you already have

Unit 4 Science Fiction I
page 43

1. Loneliness
2. The Interstellar Exploratory Fleet
3. The faraway star of Tau Ceti
4. An enormous monster with spiky fur
5. The monster had snakelike tentacles growing from its neck in place of a head.
6. Pudding being sucked from a boot
7. He believed he was having a nightmare.
8. The monsters he thought were just nightmares were real.

Answer Key

Unit 4 Science Fiction II

page 47

1. Universe Central
2. Once every ten billion years
3. As a Plynchin, Varuna carried her own ecosystem and had extra defenses against any outside forces that might disrupt her breathing or nourishment.
4. To arrive at a place
5. Varuna's new boss
6. Dinosaurs
7. Volcanic eruptions or an asteroid collision
8. Humans

Unit 5 Ancient Civilizations

page 55

1. A time when a culture or nation is at its greatest
2. The mid-400s B.C.E.
3. A tragedy is about a person who faced a very difficult decision. They have sad endings.
4. Athens had a huge outdoor theater that could fit 14,000 people. Each year a big festival was held there where plays were performed. Prizes were given out to the best plays and actors.
5. The study of wisdom
6. A famous temple in Athens built by Greek architects
7. Beautiful statues of gods, goddesses, and ordinary people.
8. Statue of Zeus at Olympia

Unit 5 Geography

page 59

1. Canada
2. Lake Ontario, Lake Erie, Lake Huron, Lake Superior
3. Atlantic, Pacific, and Arctic
4. Rocks
5. Inlets
6. A region of low, flat land
7. This area is a tundra, with the coldest temperatures and harshest landscapes in Canada.
8. The area is too cold for trees to grow.

Unit 5 Economics

page 63

1. Things that are valuable or useful to a place
2. Food, water, and shelter
3. Needs are things we must have to live. Wants are the things we enjoy having and doing.
4. The price of a product falls.
5. The price of oil would rise.
6. The use of goods and services
7. Four
8. Command economies

Common Core Comprehension Grade 6 • ©2012 Newmark Learning, LLC

Answer Key

Unit 5 Government and Citizenship

page 67

1. Africa
2. The people of Darfur are fleeing Sudan to avoid being killed by government militias and rebel groups.
3. A right to life, liberty, and equality
4. He was born in a city in Finland that was taken over by the Soviet Union. This experience motivated him to advance peace and help others in similar situations.
5. The United Nations is an organization that tries to bring nations of the world together to work for peace.
6. Slavery and other types of abuse
7. In countries where voting is not allowed, citizens who try to do so can be threatened or killed.
8. This makes sure that all citizens have a say in how their government works.

Unit 6 Life Science: Ecology

page 73

1. Fungi are plants that grow on the roots of other plants.
2. The roots of a milkweed plant get water from the fungi.
3. Sunlight, water, and nutrients to grow
4. A relationship in which both living things involved help each other
5. The bees carry the pollen from one flower to another.
6. Living things that feed off other living things and harm them
7. One example is when a leech sucks a human's blood
8. Parasites weaken their hosts, making it harder for them to survive and reproduce.

Unit 6 Environmental Science

page 77

1. Deforestation is when trees are cut down and new ones are not planted to replace them.
2. One quarter of the United States
3. Forests are being destroyed by animals and humans.
4. Forest fires happen when little rain falls, forests dry out, and lightning strikes a dry tree, starting a wildfire.
5. People destroy forests to build streets and towns. Other possible answers: wildfires, volcanoes, and hurricanes
6. Trees cut down and cleared to make way for homes, roads, malls
7. Half of the land in the United States
8. Anything that hurts living things or natural resources

Answer Key

Unit 6 Physical Science: Forces and Motion

page 81

1. A push or a pull
2. Any change in an object's or person's position
3. The muscles in a pitcher's shoulder pull on the bones of her arm. This pulling raises her arm back. Other muscles pull on bones to swing her arm forward.
4. To swing a baseball bat and hit a ball in a new direction
5. When a bat hits a ball, the bat changes the direction of the ball with a big push. This sends the ball high in the air.
6. Gravity
7. Friction, or when one surface rubs against another surface, makes a rolling ball stop. The rubbing involved in friction is the action that slows the ball down.
8. Gas particles in the air

Unit 6 Earth Science: Energy

page 85

1. The ability to do work
2. Light and heat
3. Trees use energy to grow
4. Potential energy
5. The energy of movement
6. The remains of ancient living things, coal, natural gas, and petroleum; nonrenewable resources such as fossil fuels
7. Nuclear energy
8. The sun

Unit 7 Persuasive Essays I

page 93

1. The city
2. Not possible to even think about
3. Los Angeles is large and sprawling. New York City is more concentrated with good public transportation.
4. The Boston Symphony or the Boston Pops
5. The Charles River
6. The Old North Church and Paul Revere's house are located on the trail; "How about history?"
7. The writer lives in Boston.
8. Answers will vary.

Answer Key

Unit 7 Persuasive Essays II

page 97

1. An area of living just outside of a city
2. In suburbs kids are always around other kids. Their family-centered design is also a great place for a kid to grow up.
3. Andover, Massachusetts, a suburb of Boston
4. Go to the movies, the theater, and diverse restaurants, or play on the many recreation fields
5. Just over 30,000 people
6. In the suburbs, the writer knows what every one of his neighbors looks like, they greet him by name, his parents have many friends, and his neighbors always help one another out when in need.
7. The sports facilities are never too crowded or reserved for those only with a special permit like in the city. And in the country, people live close enough to each other so that it is worthwhile for a town to build places to play sports. People never have to drive far to play organized sports, so there's always plenty of participants to play with.
8. Answers will vary.

Unit 8 Book Reviews

page 103

1. Roald Dahl
2. Her family treats her badly and her principal treats her even worse.
3. Her father breaks the law, her mother leaves her alone all day, the family sits in front of the TV all night, and dinner is always warmed-up frozen meals.
4. Crazy, very odd
5. She throws children out the window and locks them in tiny cupboards with sharp glass on the walls.
6. She is kind to everyone but does not have any backbone.
7. To convince you to read *Matilda*
8. Answers will vary.

Unit 8 Film Reviews

page 107

1. People who write movies
2. The writer says that they were funny together as Matilda's parents and they made her laugh every time.
3. A horseback-riding crop
4. He sells used cars that are lemons.
5. Matilda is a nice kid but not a pushover. For example, when her father is mean, she fights back. When she realizes her parents will not do much to help her, she is not afraid to stand up and take care of herself.
6. Smaller stories within the bigger story
7. There are scenes in which the headmaster's house appears haunted, and where the children take revenge on the headmaster and erasers attack her.
8. Yes, the writer says you'll want to watch this movie "over and over."

Answer Key

Unit 9 Advertisements I

page 113

1. A new board game called Chess Mess
2. Two hundred years old
3. The game comes equipped with four water spouts, one on each corner of the board.
4. When you check your opponent
5. You get sprayed by a water spout
6. Four
7. Each side of the board has a nozzle to fill up each spout.
8. A master chess player

Unit 9 Advertisements II

page 117

1. Having a fluttery feeling in your stomach
2. Feeling nervous or scared before a big event
3. Jelly candies
4. Butterfly-shaped
5. First you swallow a Whim Wham, then you wait a moment, and soon you'll feel a tickle in your tummy. The tickle keeps going as long as you keep eating Whim Whams.
6. Bouncing Berry, Frazzled Fruit, Sour Skittishness, or Hot Heebie-Jeebies
7. They flutter in your stomach.
8. Answers will vary.

Unit 10 Speeches I

page 123

1. People like the writer, who are engineers
2. Coal, oil, natural gas
3. Warming our homes and cooking our food
4. Solar power only makes electricity. They cannot power our means of transportation.
5. Able to do many things
6. Environmental problems like air pollution and climate change
7. Nuclear power
8. Answers will vary.

Unit 10 Speeches II

page 127

1. Three: solar, wind, water power
2. Limitless, widely available, environmentally safe
3. They are used up forever.
4. Convert sunlight to energy
5. 1/5
6. We give those countries billions of dollars to buy their fossil fuels.
7. Nuclear power
8. Answers will vary.

Notes

Notes